I count it a high honor and privilege to be able to send you this volume, written by my associate Paul Van Gorder, as a way of saying thank you for your faithful support! Paul and I have shared the responsibility of proclaiming God's Word on "Day of Discovery" and on the Radio Bible Class broadcasts for a number of years. I have been increasingly grateful for his outstanding biblical knowledge, the depth of his spiritual discernment, and his devout walk with God.

So please accept from both of us this token of our appreciation for your encouragement in the work of the Gospel through Radio Bible Class.

May God bless you!

Richard W. De Haan

The Church
Stands
Corrected

Paul R. Van Gorder

This book is designed for your personal
reading pleasure and profit. It is also designed for group study. A leader's guide
with helps and hints for teachers is available from your local Christian bookstore or
from the publisher at $1.25.

VICTOR BOOKS

a division of SP Publications, Inc.
WHEATON. ILLINOIS 60187

Scripture quotations in this book are from *The New Scofield Reference Bible,* © 1967 by the Delegates of the Oxford University Press, Inc., New York. Used by permission.

Library of Congress Catalog Card Number: 76-10505
ISBN: 0-88207-733-3

© 1976 by SP Publications, Inc. World rights reserved. Printed in the United States of America

VICTOR BOOKS
A division of SP Publications, Inc.
P.O. Box 1825 ● Wheaton, Illinois 60187

Preface

As I travel around the country, and when I read various religious periodicals, I'm increasingly concerned about the signs of carnality and the indifference to biblical truth that I observe. Denominations and individual assemblies of believers alike are failing to heed the Bible's admonition to maintain their doctrinal and moral purity, and as a result, the blessing of the Lord is lost.

Some of the very attitudes and problems being encountered today were present in the church at Corinth. I've written this analysis of 1 Corinthians, therefore, with the purpose and prayer that we might see the need for the church to cleanse itself from sin and safeguard the truths of God's holy Word.

A project like this is not done alone. I want to express sincere appreciation to my faithful secretary of many years, Mrs. Martha Brown, for her patient and valuable assistance. A word of thanks is also in order to Clair Hess, Director of Publications for Radio Bible Class, and to David Egner, for their editorial help.

Paul Van Gorder

Contents

Introduction

The church at Corinth was no different from the church at Denver, Cleveland, Edgefield, Toronto, or Boone's Creek. Those early believers were confronted by problems of conduct just as we are today. The Corinthian congregation was surrounded by a polluted and idolatrous environment, and we are faced by similar adegradation in our society.

Corinth was the capital of the province of Achaia. This great port city was known for its architecture, wealth, works of art, athletic games, and schools of philosophy. But it had one major drawback; its open and gross licentiousness. The entire city was steeped in immorality of the worst kind. It centered in the worship of the Greek goddess Aphrodite, called Venus by the Romans, the goddess of lust or carnal love. In fact, a term of evil connotation had been coined in that day, *Corinthiazesthai*, meaning simply, "to live like a Corinthian."

But God had wrought a work of grace in Corinth, principally through the ministry of the Apostle Paul. The account of his labor and success is recorded in Acts 18, where we are told that "many of the Corinthians, hearing, believed and were baptized" (Acts 18:8).

Paul sailed from Corinth to Ephesus in the company of Priscilla and Aquila. He remained there a short time before proceeding to Caesarea and on to Jerusalem. Shortly after he had departed for Palestine, the gifted orator Apollos came to Ephesus seeking further instruction in the truth. Aquila and Priscilla taught him, so that he might know "the way of God more perfectly" (Acts 18:26). Then, with a letter of introduction in hand, Apollos went to Corinth, where he preached publicly, "showing by the Scriptures that Jesus was Christ" (v. 28).

When Paul returned to Ephesus, he soon heard that the young Corinthian church was in woeful condition and in desperate need of spiritual help. The elders of Corinth had written the apostle to request instruction and information primarily on matters of Christian conduct.

Yes, personal behavior—the way we live—is important in the Christian life and witness. The Apostle's incisive letter to the Corinthian church deals forthrightly and honestly with the problems of personal and church conduct. In this book we will examine what he had to say, applying it to our situation today.

The local church, recognizing that it is part of the Body of Christ—a fellowship of believers stationed in the world and yet called out from the world—should bear consistent witness to the Lord Jesus, its living Head. The conduct of an assembly, as well as of the individual believer, is to correspond to His life. But if conduct is shaped by worldly wisdom, as was the case in Corinth, fleshly indulgence soon manifests itself in various ways. Fellowship with God is hampered, and its effectiveness is limited because of sin.

May it please the Lord to use our study of 1 Corinthians in the correction of wrong practices and the strengthening of Christian conduct, thus purifying His church.

1

Cracks of Carnality

(1 Corinthians 1:10—4:21)

A solid, perfect foundation may be designed and laid out, but this does not guarantee a building without defects. Inferior materials, improper joining of segments, or poor quality of workmanship may cause cracks to develop later. The apostle Paul said of his work at Corinth, "According to the grace of God which is given unto me, as a wise master builder, I have laid the foundation" (1 Cor. 3:10). That foundation was Jesus Christ. These to whom Paul was writing were genuine Christians, grounded upon the Solid Rock. But cracks of carnality had developed in the superstructure.

Christians at Corinth (1:1-9)
The epistle of 1 Corinthians is addressed to "the church of God which is at Corinth" (1 Cor. 1:2). The letter was sent to a local assembly, a called-out people, who had been brought into fellowship with Jesus Christ by faith, and were members of His Body, the Church.

9

The outreach of this epistle extends beyond the confines of the church at Corinth, for it is also addressed to "all that in every place call upon the name of Jesus Christ, our Lord" (1 Cor. 1:2). The principles for Christian conduct written to the church at Corinth, therefore, are applicable to the entire church, both then and now. The true circle of fellowship includes only those who have bowed to the authority of Christ, God's appointed Ruler, and who consequently are in living union with the whole body of believers. They have acknowledged that the center of their worship is not a creed, not a system, but "Jesus Christ, our Lord."

True believers have been sanctified in Christ Jesus. The author of Hebrews said this was accomplished through "the offering of the body of Jesus Christ once for all" (Heb. 10:10). This sanctification is eternal and unchanging, a correlative of the believer's position in Christ Jesus, and it depends entirely upon His merits. Christians therefore have been "set apart" or "devoted to a holy purpose," and are called "saints." They are to show forth the divine purpose of their sanctification by walking in God's holiness.

In the Church today, as in the church at Corinth, many Christians have forgotten this purpose. These opening verses (1 Cor. 1:4-9), give us as commendable a description of the saints as is ever recorded, yet no church ever received such scathing rebukes as this one. Why then did such glaring "cracks" appear in the superstructure of this church? They did not come from their past, for Paul wrote, "That in everything ye are enriched by Him" (v. 5). A message had been deposited with them and they had understood it, for Paul said, "The testimony of

Christ was confirmed in you" (v. 6). The witness of the Apostle concerning the Lord Jesus had taken root in their lives, giving real evidence of their genuine conversion. The problems also did not stem from some work of God they were lacking in the present, for the Apostle said, "that ye come behind in no gift" (v. 7). They had received all the necessary gifts of the Holy Spirit. Some among them could minister the Word acceptably, others had teaching ability, and some had miraculous gifts. But cracks of carnality had still appeared.

Further, the Apostle Paul spoke of their future expectation, saying that they were "waiting for the coming of our Lord Jesus Christ" (v. 7). They looked for the "unveiling," His personal manifestation before the world. The problem therefore wasn't from their view of the future. They had the true assurance that Christ Himself would confirm them "unto the end" (v. 8). They had the confidence "that He who hath begun a good work in you will perform it until the day of Jesus Christ" (Phil. 1:6).

So in verses 4 through 9 of chapter 1, Paul was speaking of the Corinthian Christians' *standing* in Christ; their *state* came far short of this as we shall see. The Apostle was preparing them for the harsh reproofs to follow. All of us as believers need to ask ourselves if the *state* of our Christian experience approximates our *standing* in Christ. Since we are members of His Body, since we have been sanctified, since we are called saints, great demands are placed upon us for holy conduct and consecrated living. How closely are we living up to them?

Report to the Master Builder
The Apostle Paul had been commissioned by the

risen Christ to preach the Gospel in Corinth and to found a church. He had laid that foundation, so it was perfectly proper for him to be given a progress report. For a year and a half he had labored in Corinth, "teaching the Word of God among them" (Acts 18:11). Near the end of his stay in Ephesus, the Apostle received that report. It did *not* come as an unsigned letter, for it would seem out of character for Paul to correct any church on the basis of an anonymous statement.

Members of the household of Chloe had told him there were contentions among the Christians at Corinth. They were wrangling among themselves. Therefore he wrote, "For ye are yet carnal; for whereas there is among you envying, and strife, and divisions, are ye not carnal, and walk as men?" (1 Cor. 3:3)

There was disputing—one can almost hear their comments as they leave the building where they assembled for teaching, fellowship, breaking of bread, and prayer. Some are saying, "I am of Paul." I can imagine comments like, "I like Paul; after all, he founded our church. And what a teacher!" Others, however, said, "I am of Apollos. He's a far more eloquent man, and that's for me. None of this dry teaching; give me a preacher with some flair!" Still others declared, "I am of Peter." I can just hear them, "I like Peter, he's a man of action. I'm for someone who is practical—that's what this church needs." Then, I sense an air of superiority in the cry of those who said, "I am of Christ!" Their halos are set at a jaunty angle. "Not me! I never follow any of those. I take my orders from Christ. I don't need any other Christian to tell me what to do!"

What was happening? The division probably was centered around actual men in the local assembly of believers, for the Apostle says, "And these things, brethren, I have *in a figure* transferred to myself and to Apollos for your sakes, that ye might learn in us not to think of men above that which is written, that no one of you be puffed up for one against another" (1 Cor. 4:6).

Paul was dismayed because of these factions and divisions, as any true servant of the Lord would be. Godly pastors do not desire the plaudits of their congregations, nor do they seek to rally to themselves the adulation of believers. The treacherous purpose of Satan is always to turn men's eyes away from Christ to the men who preach Him. The testimony of the church is greatly diminished in the world by the rise of disputing factions. In the first four chapters of 1 Corinthians, therefore, the Apostle Paul set forth five "cracks of carnality" which could cause divisions within any church. We will examine each of them in detail, with an eye to our own contemporary situation.

Failure to Acknowledge the Headship of Christ (1:13-16)

Paul began dealing with the problem at Corinth by asking three pertinent questions: Is Christ divided? Was Paul crucified for you? Were ye baptized in the name of Paul? They point to the first crack of carnality which causes division—an unwillingness to submit to Christ's authority.

Paul's first question, "Is Christ divided?" is thoroughly answered in 1 Corinthians 12:12-27. This passage tells us that we are members of one body, and the head of that body is Christ. As believers we have but one source of authority, one head, one object of our allegiance—Jesus Christ.

The second question brought to their minds the ground of their new life, the price paid for their redemption. Blood was shed. Whose blood? The blood of God's Lamb, His spotless Son, crucified for us.

In the third question Paul discussed the vital truth concerning baptism. Baptism is to show identification with Christ (Rom. 6:3-7), and the person who performs it is of minimal importance. The focus is to be upon our union with Christ, not upon our relationship to the person who baptized us.

When any *man* is exalted, regardless of the great spiritual influence he may wield, the place of the crucified, risen, ascended Christ is minimized. Christians, as members of the true Church which is His Body, must be drawn to the Lord Jesus. Through His death, burial, and resurrection believers are united to Him. When His headship is ignored, carnality begins to appear in the church.

Failure of Human Wisdom (1:18-25)

When Christians forget that it was the "preaching of the cross" that God used in their salvation, and become enthralled with verbal eloquence and worldly wisdom instead, carnality breaks forth within the congregation. Time and again, we have seen the Church attempt to amalgamate some attractive new philosophy into its belief-system, and the result has always been disastrous. In fact, the modernistic movement serves as a primary example. Paul asked three questions: "Where is the wise?" (In this he speaks of philosophy.) "Where is the scribe?" (This is a reference to systems of religion and ritual.) "Where is the disputer?" (This is the man of logic, of human reasoning.) None of these can fathom or imagine salvation being obtained through the death of an innocent sacrifice on a cross. For it comes, as John said, "not of blood, nor of the will of the flesh, nor of the will of man, but of God" (John 1:13).

The Gospel is not a system of philosophy, but God's means of salvation. "It pleased God by the foolishness of preaching to save them that believe" (1 Cor. 1:21). The Apostle warned another church about this by saying, "Beware lest any man spoil you through philosophy and vain deceit, after the tradition of men, after the rudiments of the world, and not after Christ" (Col. 2:8).

Wherever Christians gather, let them take heed that the wisdom of the world does not infiltrate the assembly and divide God's people. The church at Corinth, located in a city and a nation in which human wisdom had ripened and come to full fruit, was tempted to "upgrade" its position by adopting man's philosophy. The Apostle reminded them that it was the proclamation of Christ crucified and risen that had brought the power and wisdom of God to them. Carnality will be evidenced in any group of believers that exalts human wisdom in message or method.

Failure to Recognize the Constitution of the Church (1:26-31)

Class distinction is another mark of carnality. G. Campbell Morgan said that when he was a boy, people judged the influence of a church by the number of carriages drawn up outside. In some quarters, it is much the same today. Paul invites these Corinthian Christians to look over the ground; to observe carefully those who constituted their fellowship of believers; to call the roll!

Sometimes we think we would be better off if our church had more intellectuals, more people of influence and ability, more members considered by the world to be "well-born." But this is not how God works. Note the designations given by the Apostle: "Not many wise men after the flesh, not many mighty, not many noble" (v. 26). How vital for us to remember that all men are sinners, lost, hopeless, blind, dead! No one is fit to stand before a holy God. To become conceited and divisive is to deny the operation of His grace. God has used the foolish, weak, lowly things—the "things which are not"—to bring glory to Himself. Remember, these Corinthian Christians were saying, "I am of Paul, Apollos, Cephas" Wait a minute! Who is Paul anyway? Who is Apollos? Better remove the halo! Something is wrong when we begin to exalt any man or woman.

I remember that our aged, godly physician had pasted across his desk lamp these words: "But for the grace of God . . ." It is time for us to set aside all class distinctions, and to become deeply aware that we are "in Christ Jesus." To us He is "wisdom, and righteousness, and sanctification, and redemption." If God has received us, then we are to receive one another. Let no believer glory in himself or in any man. "He that glorieth, let him glory in the Lord" (v. 31).

Failure to Acknowledge the Source of Ministry (2:1-16)

The fourth "crack of carnality" which endangers

church unity is an ignoring of the truth that all effective ministry or work of the Gospel originates in God.

Two men visited church services one Sunday in London. At the morning worship hour they went to hear a renowned pulpiteer deliver an address in a beautiful cathedral. They came away saying, "What a wonderful preacher he is!" That evening they went to hear Charles Haddon Spurgeon. As they left Metropolitan Tabernacle, they remarked, "What a wonderful Christ that man preached!"

The Apostle Paul did not devote himself to rhetoric. He easily could have, for he had the vocabulary. He had been schooled in Greek rhetoric, philosophy, and literature, and could have exploited all three in the proclamation of the message. But he knew that his preaching was to be in the demonstration and power of the Spirit. The factions and splinters that prevailed in Corinth were clear indications that many of those believers were *not* acknowledging God as the source of Paul's ministry. Apart from the power of the Holy Spirit and the illumination He gives, no sinner would be able to receive or understand the Gospel. God has revealed Himself in the person of His Son, given us this revelation in His Word, and applied it through the Holy Spirit. If He had not, we would still be lost.

The Church of Jesus Christ, guarding against divisions and strife, must acknowledge that all proclamation of the truth and understanding of that truth comes only by the Spirit of God. Any minister of the Gospel is but a mouthpiece for the Holy Spirit. Making certain that our faith stands not in the wisdom of men "but in the power of God" delivers us from that divisive party spirit that exalts men, whose feet are still of clay.

Failure to Understand the Christian Ministry (3:1-5)

The fifth mark of carnality is related to the fourth. Not only must we acknowledge that the source of our salvation is God, but we must diligently keep from elevating any popular Bible teacher or preacher above the elected leadership of the church. How prone we are to divide into factions, or to exalt some Christian "hero" above the Lord Jesus! We must beware when *anyone* comes to us and says, "I have the truth for your church and can solve all your problems." The writer of Hebrews commanded: "Remember them who have the rule over you, who have spoken unto you the word of God, whose faith follow, considering the end of their manner of life" (Heb. 13:7). The teaching of 1 Corinthians 3 does not negate this in any way. Paul was simply warning that members of the church are to acknowledge the authority of the One who sent the preacher, not of the preacher himself.

In Corinth, little cliques of followers had formed around different men. Who were these men, Paul and Apollos, anyway? The Apostle answered with the word *diakonos*, which means "a minister, a servant." These men were errand boys under assignment. As servants of God, they were not the originators of a system of truth. They were not leaders of a certain party. They were not the protagonists of a particular creed. Each was to perform his own definite work as a servant of God.

Paul said, "I planted." Putting the seed into the

ground, of course, is important. But man cannot impart life to it. "All I can do is put the seed into the ground," Paul said. This he had done for a year and a half in Corinth. Then Apollos "watered." This too was necessary to growth and development. But watering alone does not give life. The secret of life is not in the man who sows, the one who plants, nor the one who waters. Listen to Paul's inspired words: "So, then, neither is he that planteth anything, neither he that watereth, but God that giveth the increase" (v. 7). I remember hearing Dr. M. R. De Haan put it this way: "Zero plus zero still equals zero."

May God help those of us who are charged with preaching and teaching the Word to have a right appraisal of our God-given ministry. And may our Lord help all who hear the Word to realize that it is "God that giveth the increase." By His power and sovereign will alone comes first the blade, then the ear, then the fully ripened corn.

Instead of being leaders of rival sects, Christ's ministers must remember they are working together under the direction of their Living Head. We do the Body harm whenever we compare different members. Each minister and leader is appointed of the Holy Spirit to his own function. The Spirit of God "divideth severally as He will." But we are one! How this must have cut the hearts of the Christians at Corinth! Think of the shame they must have felt when these words were read!

The Apostle Paul sounds a warning note by reminding all ministers that their work will one day be judged. At Corinth he had laid the proper foundation, Jesus Christ. Then he warned, "But let every man take heed how he buildeth upon it" (v.

10). An anonymous Christian writer has said, "Works done by man, through man, and to man, may bulk large in the public eye, but when tried by the fire of divine approval will pass away in smoke." The church can avoid these "cracks of carnality" by understanding that ministers of the Gospel "have this treasure in earthen vessels, that the excellency of the power may be of God, and not of us" (2 Cor. 4:7).

The Apostle's Appeal

It's examination time. Take a few minutes, friend, to consider the church where you fellowship. Is there evidence of carnality? Or do you submit constantly to the headship of Jesus Christ? Are you resorting to human wisdom? Do you receive those whom Christ has received, acknowledging that whatever you are, you are by the grace of God? Do you build with care, knowing that one day "every man's work shall be made manifest"? You must honestly confront and answer these searching questions, and if you find weakness or failure, take steps to correct it at once.

The appeal of the Apostle Paul to those Corinthian Christians is also directed to us: "Now I beseech you, brethren, by the name of our Lord Jesus Christ, that ye all speak the same thing, and that there be no divisions among you, but that ye be perfectly joined together in the same mind and in the same judgment" (1 Cor. 1:10).

2

Indifference to Immorality

(1 Corinthians 5:1-13)

The Church today is surrounded, as it was in Corinth, by a corrupt society. Materialism pervades our culture, permissiveness and pornography dominate the entertainment media, and apathy and pessimism have displaced the old-fashioned virtues of industry, self-restraint, and courage. Whenever the Church allows itself to become influenced by worldly wisdom, it begins to favor the flesh, as evidenced in the Corinthian Christians by their carnality. The flesh is the worst enemy of the believer, because it gives Satan and his cohorts a beachhead from which to extend their control over his entire life.

Taken up with the "wisdom of words," the Corinthian Christians had become careless concerning the "word of the cross." Some may say, "It doesn't make any difference what you believe, just as long as you live right." But, friend, it is impossible to *live* right unless you *believe* right. The Word is what should regulate our moral conduct. The church at Corinth tolerated immorality because it wasn't believing right, a condition which characterizes the church today.

⌐What travesty is made out of the cause of Christ and the Church which bears His name when professing Christians, some of them leaders, become slanderers, cheat their fellowmen, or commit sexual sins. No wonder many churches, with thoroughly orthodox doctrinal creeds, are in reality a pitiful spectacle of spiritual impotence. Whenever immorality and blatant, open sin are tolerated in the assembly, whenever indifference is shown toward moral conduct, spiritual degeneration is the result.

A spirit of unwillingness to follow the scriptural pattern for discipline in cases of immorality and sin have caused both the local church and the entire Body of Christ to suffer great spiritual harm. According to the Bible, a church has power in direct proportion to its purity. May every Christian who reads this chapter, even though he may consider himself free of any moral dereliction, examine himself and allow the searchlight of the Word of God to expose every sin. Just as in the church corporate, so also in the individual believer, unjudged sin brings spiritual weakness, and inevitably the displeasure of a holy God will be made known.⌐

⌐The Need for Discipline

The Apostle Paul had received word, either through someone from the household of Chloe or by a letter from a member of the assembly, that a case of flagrant immorality was going uncorrected in the church at Corinth. The text says, "It is reported commonly." The *New American Standard Bible* translates these words, "It is actually reported"

(1 Cor. 5:1). The sinful conduct of one member of the congregation was now public information. It was no longer a private sin, though that itself must be confessed and judged. It had become a matter of public reproach; it had passed the rumor stage; it was fact. Paul said, "It is reported commonly that there is fornication among you, and such fornication as is not so much as named among the Gentiles, that one should have his father's wife" (5:1).

The sin was so terrible that even among the Gentiles, the heathen society of that day, this conduct was not practiced or condoned. A man at the church at Corinth had his father's wife, that is, his stepmother. The language of the Apostle seems to imply that this woman had been divorced by the father and was now married to the son. The curse of God had always been upon deeds like this in Israel. Though we are now in the age of grace, we are still governed by the same holy God.

The general attitude of the Christians at Corinth was described by the words "puffed up." Pride had filled their hearts. How often worldly sophistication marks the church today!

The Apostle allowed for the possibility that the church leaders at Corinth did not know how to deal with this nasty problem. But he said that they could at least have "mourned" over the sin and cried out to the Lord in their sorrow. Indeed, sadness of heart and humility of mind are honored by God, and He would have responded accordingly. If they had cried out to God, He certainly would have heard them. But they were blinded by carnality and spiritual pride, and had become boastful. What dangers threaten any church that becomes too proud to deal with sin! The Corinthians boasted that they were of a certain party, or followers of a certain man, but how utterly absurd was such partisan arrogance while immorality was present among them! Instead of bragging, they should have hung their heads in mourning. If they had been really concerned, the guilty one would have been removed from their fellowship, and there would have been no need for Paul to rebuke them.

Churches should ask themselves today, "Where is the mourning? Where is the sorrow for sin in the midst of the assembly? Where is distress of soul because of open transgression in the church? Is discipline practiced, or does superficial pride keep us from confronting and purging away our wickedness?"

The Method of Discipline

Paul wrote this epistle from Ephesus, where he had been preaching and teaching the Word of God (see Acts 20:31; 1 Cor. 16:5-8). But the moment he heard of this sordid condition in the church at Corinth he passed judgment. What they should have done months before, he did at once in his own mind. He had great concern for the Corinthian believers. He was not willing to see the work he had started under the direction of the Spirit of God destroyed by a group of "puffed up" people who would not discipline a sinning brother. The Apostle says, "For I verily . . . have judged already, as though I were present, concerning him that hath done this deed" (v. 3). This was *not* a violation of Paul's directive to "judge nothing before the time" (1 Cor. 4:5). That command had nothing to do with individual judgment before knowing all the facts in the case. The situation at Corinth was totally different, for an open, public sin was affecting the entire church. Judgment was to come by action of the assembly, which should have excommunicated this man from the local church.

Paul is not dealing so much with the individual case of the man; he is more concerned with the failure of the assembly. But someone objects, saying, "Remember Galatians 6:1." Unlike one "being over-taken in a fault," however, this man had willfully been engaging in continued, open sin. His treatment was to be much different from that of a fellow believer who had been "overtaken."

Apostolic Authority

The Apostle considered himself to be a part of the Corinthian church, for "he that is joined unto the Lord is one spirit" (1 Cor. 6:17). He had already passed judgment, which was the prerogative of an apostle. In a similar case, Paul speaks of two men whom he had "delivered unto Satan, that they may learn not to blaspheme" (1 Tim. 1:20). Dr. J. Sidlow Baxter has written, "The apostles were a group of authoritatively inspired men in a category all by themselves, required for a special effort. . . . They were uniquely authorized teachers with a conferred authority strictly peculiar to themselves. What Paul the Apostle could do by that invested author-ity and supernatural insight, we cannot. Yet the incident shows what our attitude ought to be toward such sin among believers" (*Explore the Book,* Grand Rapids, Zonderan, p. 108)

Church Authority

The church at Corinth, however, did have the au-thority to discipline this man "in the name of our

Lord Jesus Christ" and "with the power of our Lord Jesus Christ" (1 Cor. 5:4). In this day, when there is a growing independence from all kinds of authority in government, school, and home, the Church must take heed lest the spirit of lawlessness seize it also. Since it is identified with the Lord Jesus Christ, the risen Head of the church, in His name and in His power the local assembly of believers must purge its fellowship and keep itself pure from sin. The Apostle commanded the church at Corinth "to deliver such an one unto Satan for the destruction of the flesh" (v. 5). As a representative of the Lord Jesus Christ (Eph. 4:11), Paul demanded action, and the church was obligated to assemble and to do what was required.

Two interpretations of the kind of judgment called for here are often presented by Bible scholars. First, the flesh had become master in the sinning man, so it is possible that the church was simply to surrender him up to it. He had already surrendered himself to the flesh anyway. In other words, they would hand him over to the dominion of Satan, and exclude him from the fellowship of the church.

I am inclined to believe, however, that this action involved physical consequences. To me, the use of the word *flesh* refers to the lusts that dwelt within the body of the man. It follows, then, that the offender was to be put into the hands of the adversary for physical affliction and ultimately for death. As F. W. Grant suggests in his commentary, "Satan can serve himself no longer by the sin of one who has been expelled from the Christian assembly. He has, therefore, nothing that he can do except to manifest his enmity against one who has borne the name of Christ, perhaps with the thought of driving him to despair by that which falls upon him or, as in Job's case, urge him into railing against God Himself. God uses him, on the other hand, that in the destruction of the flesh the spirit may yet be saved in the day of the Lord Jesus" (*The Numerical Bible:* Acts to 2 Corinthians, Loizeaux Brothers, 1901, p. 476). Further light may be given by this passage: "If any man see his brother sin a sin which is not unto death, he shall ask, and he shall give him life for them that sin not unto death. There is a sin unto death; I do not say that he shall pray for it" (1 John 5:16). This had already happened to some of the Christians at Corinth, as we shall note later. Some of them who had abused the Lord's Table and had not judged this sin in their lives were "weak and sickly . . . and many slept." God deals harshly with willful, continued, presumptuous sin, and the assembly too must purge out the old leaven. John Morley said that compromise is "the most immoral word in the English language." The government of God operating within the Church of Jesus Christ tolerates no compromise with sin—and certainly not the sins that are mentioned in this chapter.

The Reason for Discipline

But doesn't this chastening violate the parable of the wheat and tares, which were to "grow together until harvest"? No—in that parable the field is the "world"—not the church. The assembly of believers has no warrant for allowing the wicked person to remain in its fellowship. The welfare of the individual must be considered. If he is properly judged by the church, his being excluded from its fellowship may produce in him the desired effect. Paul calls for action, that "the spirit may be saved in the day of the Lord Jesus" (1 Cor. 5:5). ⟨Sinning believers are to be chastened that they might "not be condemned with the world." ⟩

Perhaps a far greater effect is to be seen in the lives of the assembled believers. The awful contagion of sin is alarming. Nothing is like it! In the physical realm, for example, most of our states have strict quarantine laws. The health officer comes and attaches a card to the door, barring entrance to that house by outsiders while confining the diseased within. The physical health of society is therefore maintained by such laws. In a similar way, the rotten apple is removed from the barrel or basket lest the other apples become spotted and spoiled. The Apostle says, "Know ye not that a little leaven leaveneth the whole lump?" (1 Cor. 5:6). Remember, Achan's sin brought the entire camp of Israel to defeat. The disobedience of that one man brought God's displeasure upon the whole nation, and the consequence serves as a warning to all ages.

The Apostle confirmed the need for the church to keep itself pure when he said, "Purge out, therefore, the old leaven, that ye may be a new lump, as ye are unleavened. For even Christ, our passover, is sacrificed for us. Therefore, let us keep the feast, not with old leaven, neither with the leaven of malice and wickedness, but with the unleavened bread of sincerity and truth" (vv. 7-8).

The Apostle mentioned the Passover and the Feast of Unleavened Bread, which were regularly observed in Israel. The blood of the lamb protected the Israelites and "made them nigh," as the death of the Lamb of God brings us into fellowship with Him.

The Feast of Unleavened Bread was always celebrated in conjunction with the Passover and speaks of fellowship maintained in holiness on the basis of the applied blood. To celebrate that feast, every Israelite cleared from his home all leaven, which always signifies evil in the Word of God. The death of the Passover lamb obligated the Israelite to search every part of his house for leaven. The Israelite was committed to put away the old bread and bring the new. In the same manner, the death of our Lord—His shed blood—makes it mandatory for us to put away sin. This is true both individually and corporately in the church. Discipline is for the purification of the local assembly.)

Grounds for Discipline (vv. 9-11)

Paul is more stringent about separation from sin among the people of the Lord than he is about keeping away from those in the world who engage in the same sin. Why? Because professing the name of Christ seems to make the sin more terrible and hideous. He says we are not to keep company with Christians who are willfully transgressing against God. This not only excludes them from the fellowship of the church, but restricts social contact with them outside of the church. We are not to mingle with them in any way.

In an epistle no longer extant, Paul had previously warned against associating with those who live sinfully (vv. 9-11). He includes as grounds for discipline not only the sin of fornication, or licentiousness, but also covetousness, idolatry, railing, drunkenness, and extortion.

Fornication is the mark of this immoral age in which we live. It eats away at the vitals of society. If one engaged in this sin is allowed to remain in the fellowship of the church, great havoc may be wrought in his or her personal life, as well as in the corporate life of the church.

Covetousness is the sin of greed. It is committed by one who has all he needs but is greedy to gain even more.

Idolatry refers especially to the worship of false gods. This too has a direct application to the present, for many today bow before "gods" of materialism, fame, or power.

Extortion is a cruel sin, for it speaks of those who swindle and rob others of what is theirs. It is motivated by a rapacious appetite, for the phrase "ravening wolves" in Matthew 7:15 is a translation of the same word.

Railing applies to slander and abusive speech, and means "vituperation, vilification, and reproach." This has to do with the harsh, cruel sins of the tongue against another person. It is noteworthy that the term often occurs with the word translated "drunkenness." A church should never permit the abusive "character assassin" to remain in its fellowship. He should either repent or be expulsed from the membership. The Apostle puts the responsibility squarely upon the congregation to shun this individual, just as it was to stay away from an incestuous person.

Drunkenness, the final sin mentioned in this list, also requires the discipline of the assembly.

The instructions are very clear and dogmatic. The church is given no recourse but to obey them. But tragically, this command which Paul states so positively is the least practiced in the church today. There is always the fear of "offending someone." Also, those who are called upon to exercise this authority are sometimes guilty themselves, or some member of their immediate family, and therefore their hands are tied. As a result, the Word of God is violated and the church is made corrupt. Instead of having genuine spiritual vitality, it is anemic and helpless.

Certainly the church, in practicing discipline, must not go beyond the bounds of the Word of God. I know a few churches that conscientiously purge out sin, and they evidence a vibrancy of spiritual health. Because the early church practiced discipline, God's power was upon it, and in a few short years it shook the foundations of the Roman empire.

A friend of mine went with a missionary one Sunday morning to visit a large assembly of believing Indians in Mexico. As they approached the open building that housed this gathering, my friend noticed two Indian men sitting on a bench outside of the church. Others were going directly under the shelter to engage in the worship and fellowship at the Lord's Table. These two men sat crying as other believers passed them by without even acknowledging their presence. My preacher friend asked the missionary what was happening. He was told that these two men, both Christians, had committed moral sins, and in the New Testament manner they had been temporarily excluded from the fellowship of the church. The disciplinary action had taken the desired effect, and the true repentance could readily be seen. "Soon," said the missionary, "they will be back in the assembly."

Does It Pay to Discipline?

The beneficial effect the discipline had on the erring man of 1 Corinthians 5 is recorded in 2 Corinthians 6—8. When it does not result in such repentance, confession, and forsaking of the sin, there is cause to believe the expelled one was never born again. My father used to say, "Discipline a sheep and it will come back to the fold bleating to be let in; discipline a hog and it will turn around and try to root down the alley, eating tin cans and garbage."

A desired and beneficial effect not only occurred in the life of the sinning believer, there also came a self-searching of the assembly in the exercise of discipline. Paul says, "For behold this very same thing, that ye sorrowed after a godly sort, what carefulness it wrought in you, yea, what clearing of yourselves, yea, what indignation, yea, what fear, yea, what vehement desire, yea, what zeal, yea, what full punishment! In all things ye have proved yourselves to be clear in this matter" (2 Cor. 7:11).

Conclusion

Let the church of Jesus Christ consider once again the biblical authority for church discipline and prayerfully seek to exercise it. Let there not be willful display, but rather a manifestation of the scriptural principle of being pure, carried out in the spirit of Christ. The limits of the Word of God must *not* be overstepped. All selfish interests must be avoided. Adhering strictly to the Bible and seeking the mind of God are sure guarantees against mistakes and abuse.

Christian friend, if there is sin in your life,

though it may be unknown by anyone in your church, take the scriptural route and "confess" that sin (1 John 1:9), lest it break out in flagrant transgression, dishonor the Lord Jesus Christ, and impede the spiritual power of His church. *⌡*

3

Correction for Contention

(1 Corinthians 6:1-8)

Some months ago the newspaper told the ugly story. Litigation was before the court, brought by deacons against a pastor, to remove him from his position and bar him from using the church facilities for his office and home. He in turn had filed a countersuit asking the court to force the church to pay his back salary. I think the newspaper must have gained a new subscriber with that issue—Satan! With gleeful delight he must have viewed the account spread across that page.

In Paul's day no newspapers carried the stories, but nevertheless the Corinthians were also airing their differences in the civil courts of their city. The issue perhaps involved the divisions over personalities, or the sinning person mentioned in the previous chapter of our study, or some other controversy not mentioned. Regardless of the subject of disagreement, however, they had brought the cause of Christ into reproach. At the root of the trouble was the problem of carnality Paul had referred to earlier when he wrote, "For ye are yet carnal; for whereas there is among you envying, and strife, and divisions, are ye not carnal, and walk as men?" (1 Cor. 3:3)

Compounding their sin was the fact that the issues being taken to court were actually of little consequence. Even the "smallest matters" were being displayed before unbelievers in a court presided over by heathen judges!

The Apostle's admonitions in 1 Corinthians 6:1-8 are therefore of considerable practical value, not alone in the matter of lawsuits of believers against believers, but contention of any nature. This is true, first of all, because the whole church is affected. Paul declared, "Whether one member suffer, all the members suffer with it; or one member be honored, all the members rejoice with it" (1 Cor. 12:26). Second, bickering and strife always bring reproach to the name of Christ. More often than not, the disagreements in the church are not over an important doctrine. Consider the splits among fundamental believers. What are they about? Usually not the result of theological disagreement or serious immoral behavior, but inconsequential matters or personality differences. The devil exploits such strife within the Church, and the cause of Christ suffers. Often the world would not have known of these contentions among Christians if they had simply obeyed the teaching of the Apostle on this subject and settled it among themselves.

Paul's Inquiry

This section begins with Paul's question, "Dare any of you . . ." He is really saying, "Do you have the courage?" The Apostle expressed amazement that a Christian would take his brother to court.

Word emphasis is always an interesting study. I recall that our freshman speech class teacher told us to repeat a sentence and change the stress from one word to another. I think I would underscore the pronoun "you" in this question. Paul asks, "Dare any of *you* . . .?" Oh, think of it, *you*—a Christian —taking differences with your brethren before heathen tribunals! Who were the "you" to whom Paul speaks? They were members of "the church of God . . ., sanctified in Christ Jesus, called to be saints" (1 Cor. 1:2). They had been "called unto the fellowship of His Son" (1 Cor. 1:9). Indeed, Paul was amazed that people of this spiritual pedigree would do such a thing. How unlike the church at its beginning, of whom we are told, "And the multitude of those that believed were of one heart and of one soul; neither said any of them that any of the things which he possessed was his own; but they had all things common" (Acts 4:32). Along a similar vein, the author of Hebrews commanded, "Follow peace with all men, and holiness, without which no man shall see the Lord; looking diligently lest any man fail of the grace of God, lest any root of bitterness springing up trouble you, and by it many be defiled" (Heb. 12:14-15). Paul may well have been recalling what had happened in Corinth while he was there (Acts 18:12-16). The unbelieving Jews had turned against him and brought him before Gallio's judgment seat. But this Gentile magistrate had refused to judge Paul in matters pertaining to Jewish tradition and practice. That heathen judge had displayed more equity in handling that matter than these Corinthians were showing to one another in their disputes! Paul would later remind these Corinthian Christians that "God is not the author of confusion but of peace, as in all churches of the saints" (1 Cor. 14:33).

The question "Dare any of you?" implied several things. If differences existed among the believers, it was evidence that (1) they were out of fellowship with God, (2) they were going to the wrong source to settle their disputes, and (3) a lawlessness was prevalent in their hearts and in the assembly. Paul wrote to Timothy, "Knowing this, that the law is not made for a righteous man but for the lawless and disobedient" (1 Tim. 1:9).

What a devastating effect their bickering must have had upon their testimony before the world! Can't you hear the comments? "Those Christians! Ha! Ha! They can't agree among themselves, so they come to us to settle their quarrels." As a result, the church was being mocked, the Lord Jesus' name was reproached, and the Gospel was made to appear a lie!

A Future Judgment

In dealing with the problem, the Apostle Paul asked the Christians at Corinth two key questions. The first was, "Do ye not know that the saints shall judge the world?" (1 Cor. 6:2) At some future day, all the world will stand on trial before Jesus Christ, and believers will be associated with Him in that judgment. Matthew 25:31-46 gives us a preview. How utterly ridiculous, therefore, that believers would carry their differences to the world's tribunals, when they themselves were destined to sit in judgment upon all mankind! The implication of Paul's question was that they either did not know of their future role, or if they did, that knowledge had not produced the desired effect in their lives.

This points up the danger of trafficking in unpracticed truth. For most of us, the problem is not a deficiency of knowledge, but rather a failure to apply that knowledge to life. We have been called "out of darkness into His marvelous light," and have been given spiritual illumination to determine our walk, our manner of living. We must *use* the knowledge that is ours!

Paul's second question was, "Know ye not that we shall judge angels?" (v. 3). This verse lets us in on a secret of which little is said in the Scriptures. In our association with the Lord Jesus, we shall have ultimate authority, not only over humanity, but over all created beings—angels included. We read in 2 Peter 2:4 and Jude 6 that there are fallen angels who are "reserved for judgment." Think of it! Believers will *judge* angels! This truth must have brought shame to the hearts of those Corinthian Christians who were trying to settle their disputes before civil magistrates. Should not believers, who are of such an exalted position that they will try the angels, be able to settle things pertaining to *this life?*

The Remedy (vv. 4-7)

These contentions and disagreements had made a mockery of the church at Corinth. How often congregations today would merit these same words of condemnation by the Apostle: "I speak to your shame." Paul suggested that if there were differences to be decided among believers, they should appoint some impartial mediator from among themselves to settle it. Whom should they choose? The least esteemed? Paul says, "Do you set them to judge?" (v. 4) This verse may be interpreted in several ways. It can be seen as a command to use such people in the assembly as arbiters in these contentions. Or the Apostle could have been using these words as a question, "Is it your custom to have this kind of person settle these matters?" This would indicate that if their disputes were not to be put before "the least esteemed" in the assembly, then certainly they should not be brought before the heathen, who in points of moral perception were certainly below these members of the church. I am inclined to think that this was Paul's way of saying that the issues involved did not require extraordinary spirituality or ability to decide. How ridiculous, then, that they should have been taken to heathen judges!

Our Lord had already given the rule for obtaining justice if a trespass is committed by one Christian brother against another.

Moreover, if thy brother shall trespass against thee, go and tell him his fault between thee and him alone; if he shall hear thee, thou hast gained thy brother. But if he will not hear thee, then take with thee one or two more, that in the mouth of two or three witnesses every word may be established. And if he shall neglect to hear them, tell it unto the church; but if he neglect to hear the church, let him be unto thee as an heathen man and a tax collector (Matt. 18:15-17).

First, the one against whom the trespass is committed is to go to his brother privately. The purpose is not to scold your fellow Christian or to "give him a piece of your mind," but to "gain your brother." But if this approach is not successful, you are to go to him and take one or two reliable members of the Body of Christ with you, so that "in the mouth of two or three witnesses every word may be established."

In our Lord's provision every attempt was made to keep the matter in as small a circle as possible. How unlike our attitudes and procedures today! Rather than directly approaching our brother, so often we go first to other Christians and air our grievances. Sadly, some even broadcast their complaints to unbelievers which only enlarges the circle of distress.

But if after going directly to your brother, and then taking one or two others with you, he should still stubbornly refuse to settle the matter, you are responsible to make further appeal. Finally, if the second attempt is fruitless, the matter must be taken to the church. But suppose one of the parties is unwilling to abide by the pattern laid down by our Lord and restated here by the Apostle in 1 Corinthians 6, what then? The Lord Jesus says that the offender must not be treated as a Christian (though he may possibly be one), but as "an heathen man and a tax collector" (Matt. 18:17).

There is an alternative suggested by the Apostle in this passage. Rather than going to law, rather than insisting on "your rights" and asserting your demands, Paul asks, "Why do ye not rather take wrong? Why do ye not rather allow yourselves to be defrauded?" (1 Cor. 6:7). He says, if all else fails, we should be willing to suffer the wrong and take the consequences. After all, God keeps the score! The writer of Proverbs suggests, "Say not thou, I will recompense evil; but wait on the Lord, and He shall save thee" (Prov. 20:22).

It is dishonoring to the Lord for a Christian to

"air his dirty linens" before the world. We are children in the same family, we are members of the same Body, we are bound together in the same life. The Bible therefore commands us,

Let all bitterness, and wrath, and anger, and clamor, and evil speaking, be put away from you, with all malice; and be ye kind one to another, tenderhearted, forgiving one another, even as God, for Christ's sake, hath forgiven you (Eph. 4:31-32).

A spirit of "getting even" by foul means or fair should never be part of the Christian's character!

Perhaps in your assembly of believers there are serious contentions. Let God's people come again to the one rule of faith and practice—the Word of God. If you personally are involved in a dispute, agree right now with God to follow *His* pattern for solving these difficulties. No longer seek *your* rights —rather, seek *Christ's* glory.

A Christian brother told that both he and Dr. M. R. De Haan were once present at a funeral. In previous years he and Dr. De Haan had had some misunderstanding, and bitterness had developed between them. My friend told me that at the close of that funeral service, he felt an arm slipped around his shoulders, and he turned to look into the face of Dr. De Haan. Calling him by name, the doctor said, "Don't you think it's time we made up, before we go to the other side?" And those two Christian men embraced and wept as fellowship between them was restored. And God was highly honored!

What renewed spiritual health would prevail among the assembly of believers if this scriptural pattern were followed! Let us consider our holy calling. Remember, we are "brethren."

4

Sin Against Sanctity

(1 Corinthians 6:9-20)

Corinth, restored by Julius Caesar and given the status of a Roman colony, had developed a terrible reputation for wantonness. Both a seat of government and a center of commerce, the city had attracted the very worst that evil men could devise —a religion of which sexual vice was a part. Immorality and perversion actually constituted a part of their worship of the goddess Aphrodite.

Many Corinthian believers in Christ had just recently been converted and had given up participation in these sinful practices. These sins of the flesh dishonored the body, and Paul included a fearful list of them: "Know ye not that the unrighteous shall not inherit the kingdom of God? Be not deceived: neither fornicators, nor idolaters, nor adulterers, nor effeminate, nor abusers of themselves with mankind, nor thieves, nor covetous, nor drunkards, nor revilers, nor extortioners, shall inherit the kingdom of God" (1 Cor. 6:9-10).

Some of this wicked city's sexual immorality had

even invaded the church, we learn from 2 Corinthians 12:20-21. Paul was expressing a deep concern for the church when he said, "For I fear lest,
when I come again . . . that I shall bewail many
who have sinned already, and have not repented
of the uncleanness and fornication and lascivious-
ness which they have committed" (2 Cor. 12:21).

So Paul asked the believers in Corinth, "Know
ye not?" (1 Cor. 6:9) He warned that God would
never tolerate uncleanness in His kingdom! One
who professes faith in Christ cannot condone sin
and still plead "grace." F. W. Grant has written,

Grace is that which breaks the dominion of sin, sets
the soul right to go on with God; and if this be not the
result of it, grace has not been learned at all, nor can it
be pleaded as availing in behalf of those who, whatever
they may profess, show themselves uninfluenced by it
(*The Numerical Bible:* Acts to II Corinthians, p. 479).

In this compromising age, when professing Christians look lightly at sin and the church is prone to
be soft on the question of moral purity, we too must
consider Paul's words, "Know ye not that the unrighteous shall not inherit the kingdom of God?"
(1 Cor. 6:9)

Past Condition and Present Position (v. 11)
Having described the tenor of the Corinthian society by naming the horrible sins practiced there,
the Apostle told the believers not to forget that
they themselves had done these things in the past.
He says, "Such were some of you." They had lived
among those conditions, and some had given themselves over to practicing gross immorality. But
something had happened! They had received the
Gospel and had been given new life, and now they

were changed. As "new creatures in Christ Jesus," they were different people. Paul used three phrases in verse 11 to describe their transformation:

1. "Ye are washed." This in no way represents water baptism, but rather the cleansing of regeneration. "Not by works of righteousness which we have done, but according to His mercy He saved us, by *the washing of regeneration,* and renewing of the Holy Spirit" (Titus 3:5). The washing came first—the removal of the defilement of sin. We have often heard men thank God that they are not what they once were. This is a good practice. The Apostle Paul never forgot that he had been "a blasphemer, and a persecutor, and injurious"; but he added, "I obtained mercy, because I did it ignorantly in unbelief" (1 Tim. 1:13). When Paul said to the Corinthians, "Such were some of you," it was right after he had enumerated the terrible sins of their city—sins of a far worse character than anything he had ever committed. But he had also said, "Christ Jesus came into the world to save sinners, of whom I am chief" (1 Tim. 1:15). So he himself was a pattern of grace. Whether we were zealous religionists like Paul or licentious, overt sinners like some of these Corinthians, every one of us who has been born of God has been washed, sanctified, and justified. The receiving of the divine nature in the new birth is the washing of regeneration.

2. "Ye are sanctified." Sin does two things: It makes us unholy and it makes us guilty. When we receive Christ, not only are we "washed," but we also are sanctified, ("set apart"), by the offering of Jesus Christ once for all. First Peter 1:2 states that we have been set apart through the "sanctification

of the Spirit." The Holy Spirit takes up His abode in us, thus making us fit to be "partakers of the inheritance of the saints in light" (Col. 1:12). We now belong to God. (As citizens of Heaven, we are but strangers and pilgrims on this earth.)

(3. "Ye are justified." When we confess our faith in Jesus, the guilt of our sin is removed and we stand justified before the throne of God. We are cleared of all sin, for we have been "declared righteous." Paul told the Romans, "Much more then, being now justified by His blood, we shall be saved from wrath through Him" (Rom. 5:9). Yes, we are declared righteous, for the sinlessness of Christ is imputed to us. We are free from all condemnation.)

My friend, the new life we received when we were born from above includes all the benefits of Christ's death, so that we can confidently say we are *washed, sanctified,* and *justified.* These blessings fully belonged to the Corinthian Christians, and they are ours as well. This is true of every believer, and Paul tells us that they were made possible through "the name of the Lord Jesus, and by the Spirit of our God" (v. 11). How thankful we can be for the glorious new life we have in Christ!)

The Christian Principle (v. 12)

(But with regeneration comes the responsibility to walk in holiness,) and this was difficult in Corinth. Remember, fornication was rampant in that city. It was common practice, and was not considered sinful by the Corinthian philosophers and teachers. Because Corinth had become the center of the worship of Aphrodite, the goddess of sensual love, this sin had actually been incorporated into the religious ritual. As mentioned, licentious rites including perversion were a regular part of their pagan worship. The scenes of lust and debauchery evidenced in those heathen temples are almost unbelievable to our modern minds!

Paul realized that these Christians were surrounded by an evil and perverted atmosphere, and that some of them had been removed from it only a short time before. He was therefore concerned with the effect upon the church. The tendency toward *toleration* of overt sin brought special spiritual anxiety to his heart, so he set forth several principles to be followed. The first was, *"All things are lawful unto me"* (v. 12). He began with the reminder that salvation is not by law, but by grace. He reiterated this basic truth later in the epistle, when he said, "All things are lawful for me, but all things are not expedient; all things are lawful for me, but all things edify not" (1 Cor. 10:23).

(But the fact that the Christian is free from the law does *not* change God's eternal moral principle.) Paul was emphasizing the liberty of the Christian life, saying "I am not under law. I am not bound." The believer should understand that he is not under any bondage to works. The Christian life is not a series of prohibitions. The Apostle Paul was not, nor are we, under a system of legalism that says, "Touch not; taste not; handle not" (Col. 2:21). Rather, ours is a marvelous liberty in Christ Jesus!

Even though we are free from all legalistic demands, we are still morally obligated to the Lord. The point in question here was particularly the use of the body. Remember, fornication was a common sin at Corinth. The Corinthians defended this practice by arguing that since God had created their bodies with sexual appetites, it was all right to use their bodies in any manner to satisfy these desires.

The course of their ill-placed logic is evident from verse 13. They reasoned: "God made the digestive organs and also made food. Therefore, food for the body, and the body for food." They applied the same reasoning to sexuality, arriving at the wrong conclusion. If to eat food is not wrong, they reasoned, then it is also not wrong to enter into promiscuous sexual relations, for God provided for both. Paul corrects their terrible error by showing that under certain circumstances even "lawful things" may not be right for the Christian (v. 12).

The second principle Paul set forth is this: "*All thing are not expedient.*" That is to say, the Christian has liberty but not license. The word "expedient" comes from the Greek verb *sumphero,* which means "bearing together." All things are lawful to me, Paul says, but *I must remember that I am not alone in the world.* This is it! *This* should govern all the conduct of the believer! Things may be perfectly lawful for me, but if they will not help my fellowship with other believers, they are to be avoided. This limitation is peculiarly Christian— not found in the religions of the world. The Corinthian believers, coming as they did out of a pagan religion influenced by a godless philosophy, were in danger of not understanding that God demands holiness and purity in the physical life.

No one questions that the believer has full and absolute freedom in the matter of eating food; yet even in this there might be things inexpedient or unprofitable. Paul warned the Romans, "But if thy brother be grieved with thy food, now walkest thou not in love. Destroy not him with thy food, for whom Christ died" (Rom. 14:15). In the use of his body, it is extremely important that the believer ask himself, "What effect would this deed have on others if I should indulge in it?" That which we allow ourselves within the scope of things entirely lawful may nevertheless have a detrimental effect upon other believers, as well as upon us.

The third principle Paul proposed is, *"I will not be brought under the power of any."* It is startling, but nonetheless true, that harmless or lawful practices may sometimes gain the mastery over us. Taking a social drink, occasionally being a glutton, indulging in some habit excused by the Christian's claim, "I am a free man," may bring great spiritual harm to others. But it also may forge another link that will bring the Christian himself under the domination of a habit, "another master." A wise saying goes, "Indulgence in unlawful things has slain its thousands, but wrong indulgence in lawful things has slain its tens of thousands." What havoc has been wrought in the lives of Christians who have indulged in some seemingly harmless practice, only to discover to their dismay and defeat that it has gained mastery over them!

The Predominant Truth (vv. 13-20)

None of the world's great religions has such lofty precepts. Only Christianity gives to mankind the exalted position expressed by the words, "Now the body is not for fornication, *but for the Lord; and the Lord for the body*" (v. 13). An explanation of this truth will answer some plaguing questions that confront many believers. The Christian's body as well as his soul is the property of the Lord.

I can imagine my reaction if some morning I should awaken to find that my neighbor had built a fence in the corner of my front yard and moved in some hogs! Then it begins to rain! In a few hours, my rich green turf is turned into a slough of mud and filth. My outrage would certainly be justified. To use the property of another against his consent and for purposes which are dishonoring to him is both inconsiderate and illegal.

⌐In the same manner, the body of the believer is not his; it belongs to the Lord. This truth is amplified by the apostle's question, "Know ye not that your bodies are the members of Christ?" (v. 15) We know that believers are members of Christ, members of His Body. But here is a different mode of speech—our bodies are His members. They belong to Him.⌐ This is the reason for Paul's plea of Romans 12: "I beseech you therefore, brethren, by the mercies of God, that ye present *your bodies* a living sacrifice, holy, acceptable unto God, which is your reasonable service. And be not conformed to this world, but be ye transformed by the renewing of your mind, that ye may prove what is that good, and acceptable, and perfect, will of God"⌐ (Rom. 12:1-2).

Furthermore we will not be done with this body when we die. Transformed, it will be ours forever in the resurrection. P. B. Fitzwater has said, "That which God so honors as not to allow it to remain forever in humiliation should receive most careful attention from us. Christ has redeemed both parts of our nature; the body has its share in the great salvation."

The Christian's body (a member of Christ, redeemed by His purchase at Calvary, and someday to be glorified) must be used here on earth to bring honor to Him. To consider taking that which belongs to Christ and engaging it in fornication is unthinkable! The Apostle cried out, "God forbid," or "May it never be!" Perish the thought that one of Christ's members should be joined to impurity or uncleanness!)

Augustine was walking in the section of a city where in earlier days he had been a profligate. When a former woman companion saw him, Augustine started to run. She called out, "Augustine, why do you run? It is only I." He looked back and answered, "I run because it is *not I.*" With this he quickened his pace and put distance between himself and the old temptation. Paul said, "I am crucified with Christ: nevertheless I live; yet not I, but Christ liveth in me" (Gal. 2:20). He commanded the Corinthians: "Flee fornication. Every sin that a man doeth is outside the body; but he that committeth fornication sinneth against his own body" (v. 18). Andrew Murray said, "The tabernacle with its wood, the temple with its stone, were as holy as all included within their walls: God's holy ones need the body to be holy.")

The Temple of the Holy Spirit (v.19)

What incisive questions are introduced to these Corinthian Christians by the words, ("Do you not know?") Here is another: ("Know ye not that your body is the temple of the Holy Spirit who is in you, whom ye have of God, and ye are not your own?") (1 Cor. 6:19) In the *body* of the believer the Spirit of God takes up His abode! Equally true is the statement of 1 Corinthians 3:16, ("Know ye not that ye are the temple of God?") In this passage the

Apostle was speaking of the church as the temple of God. But now in chapter 6 he speaks of the individual believer as the temple, the sanctuary of the Holy Spirit. The hymnwriter expressed it in this way:

> Out of dust Thy word creative
> Formed the house in which I dwell,
> And the wonder of its being
> Neither tongue nor pen can tell.
> Flesh and blood and brain together,
> In a unity sublime,
> Thou didst make to be my dwelling
> In this sunlit vale of time.
> Teach me how to make my body
> Worthy of Thee, Guest divine;
> May I keep it clean and wholesome,
> Strong and supple, straight and fine.
> Free from sloth, excess, and passion,
> May it consecrated be,
> In devoted, joyous service,
> To Thy Kingdom and to Thee.
> —Thomas Tiplady in *Hymns of Faith*

We take great care of our church buildings. The sanctuary is maintained with special attention to its cleanliness and order. A high degree of reverence is shown for what we commonly call "God's house." But the Lord "dwelleth not in temples made with hands" (Acts 17:24). How marvelous that God the Spirit dwells within the body of every believer! How the Spirit must be grieved by many of the uses to which the Christian body is subjected! Defiling the body by fornication is an awful sacrilege. To defile the body is to insult the One who lives within. When this truth is fully apprehended, much of the controversy about questionable things is removed.)

There is absolutely no excuse for a filthy home. The family may be humble and be forced to go without many of the necessities of life, but soap and water are always available. The children may have to wear patched clothes, but they do not need to wear dirty ones. Regardless of humble circumstances, the absence of talent, or the lack of learning opportunities, the believer's body is still the temple of the Holy Spirit; God dwells in him! He is to maintain that temple in purity and holiness.)

Not Our Own Anymore (vv. 19-20)
Twice in this epistle the apostle Paul by inspiration of the Spirit of God said that we are ("bought with a price.")"For ye are *bought with a price;* therefore, glorify God in your body" (6:20). "Ye are *bought with a price;* be not ye servants of men") (7:23). Dare anyone who has been redeemed at such cost, anyone who has trusted in that great price which was paid for him, live unto himself? The Lord Jesus purchased us with His own blood. The curse of judgment came upon His head! Our every sin has been fully paid. And by that price Christ has brought us to the heavenly Father. The Son has given His life, and now our life is hidden with Christ in God. The Holy Spirit has come and has made our bodies His temple, and He has sealed us. We are not our own! We have been bought with a price!)

We value things by what they cost. When we consider the price of our redemption, and estimate the value of our bodies in light of that, we will guard our purity with a holy jealousy! "Forasmuch as ye know that ye were not redeemed with corruptible things, like silver and gold . . . , but with the precious blood of Christ, as of a lamb without blemish and without spot" (1 Peter 1:18-19)

One Christian writer commented: "Our bodies are the property of Him who has purchased us at such a cost; for He did not buy us partly, but entirely. Let then the God of mercy have the willing service of those bodies which are His. The fleeting days of our sojourn here below are our opportunity of glorifying Him, by yielding ourselves to Him as those that are alive from the dead, and our members as instruments of righteousness unto God."

The Christian, realizing that his body belongs to the Lord, that the body will be resurrected, that the body is a member of Christ, that the body is the temple of the Holy Spirit, and that the body has been redeemed by the blood of Christ, will heed the command of the Apostle, "Therefore, glorify God in your body" (1 Cor. 6:20).

5

Managing the Marriage

1 Corinthians 7:1-16

The church in America is encompassed by a moral climate like that which confronted the church at Corinth. I read recently, "Ideally, the typical American family consists of one mother, one father, and two or three children. But the ideal is not true of more than one-third of all the families in the United States. Divorces, separations, desertions, and death cause one out of every three families to have a single parent. . . . This means that there are several million children growing up seeking and needing adult guidance, but who are limited to one parent" (James W. Reapsome, *Discern the Times*). The complications caused by a spiraling divorce rate are immeasurable. Information from the National Center for Health Statistics indicates a more than 70 percent increase in the last 10 years, with more than a million divorces reported in 1975.

The oldest institution in the world is the family. It is, in fact, the foundation stone of every society. Marriage was instituted by God at the beginning of the race. The purity of society and the nation is dependent upon the moral quality of its homes, and the basis of the home is the marriage. That which is treated so frivolously today, therefore, is one of the most important elements in the entire realm of Christian ethics.

The Apostle Paul, in 1 Corinthians 7, was evidently responding to a letter containing questions about the marriage relationship, especially as it affects the children of God, the church of Jesus. Since the conditions in Corinth so closely parallel those of today, Paul's answers are especially important to us, so we will examine them carefully in this chapter.

God's Order: Monogamy (7:1-2)

God intended that man and woman should marry. By the direct creative act of God, both "male and female" compose the race (Gen. 1:27). The Lord could have continued to create people by direct action as in the case of Adam, but instead He gave the power of procreation to the race. The entire teaching in the Bible is one man for one woman and one woman for one man. This is conjugal love, and the Scriptures teach that any sexual involvement outside of the lawful marriage contract is sin. The writer of Proverbs stated, "Whoso findeth a wife findeth a good thing, and obtaineth favor from the Lord" (Prov. 18:22). The Apostle Paul, in that spiritually fragrant portion on husbands and wives in Ephesians 5, said, "So ought men to love their wives as their own bodies. He that loveth his wife loveth himself" (Eph. 5:28). He later advised, "Nevertheless, let every one of you in particular so love his wife even as himself; and the wife, see that she reverence her husband" (Eph. 5:33).

The sanctity of the marriage relationship is being set aside by the easy divorce procedures of our day. It is not uncommon to see married people keeping steady company with the one he or she expects to marry as soon as a divorce is obtained. This is lust—not love.

A Mutual Relationship (7:3-5)

With the union in marriage comes mutual surrender of individualities and uniting of the virtues of both parties. They are no longer two, but one. The Lord Jesus repeatedly declared this, saying on one occasion, "For this cause shall a man leave father and mother, and shall cleave to his wife, and they two shall be one flesh" (Matt. 19:5). A surrender of individuality for both husband and wife occurs with their union in marriage. For the husband, there is to be reason and reverence; otherwise God will not answer his prayers (1 Peter 3:7). The wife is required to be in subjection, to be pure, and to be modest. The Bible describes the mutual relationship of husband and wife here in 1 Corinthians 7, in Ephesians 5, and in 1 Peter 3.

The Rule and the Possibility (7:10-11)

The teaching of the Word of God about divorce or separation is given here in verses 10 and 11. "And unto the married I command, yet not I, but the Lord, Let not the wife depart from her husband; but and if she depart, let her remain unmarried, or be reconciled to her husband, and let not the husband put away his wife" (1 Cor. 7:10-11). The Apostle Paul first indicated that the Lord Jesus Christ had already spoken on this issue, for he said,

"I command, yet not I, but the Lord." Paul's inspired word was not in conflict with that which Christ had already spoken, as recorded in Matthew 19:3-9, but was in total agreement. Our Lord was responding to a subtle question posed by the Pharisees. From the beginning of the race until the time of Moses, God made no provision for divorce. Moses' decree, stated in Deuteronomy 24, had not altered God's original purpose that one man and one woman should become one flesh and continue so until their relationship was severed by death. Moses *permitted* divorce in *Israel* "because of the hardness of their hearts." Divorce, therefore, was never sanctioned or approved by God. Christ taught that nothing dissolves the marriage relationship but death. He said, "Whosoever shall put away his wife, and marry another, committeth adultery against her. And if a woman shall put away her husband, and be married to another, she committeth adultery" (Mark 10:11-12).

This basic truth, which had been God's order from the beginning, is reiterated by the Apostle Paul. He wrote, "Let not the wife depart from her husband," and then added, "Let not the husband put away his wife" (1 Cor. 7:10-11). Nothing could be clearer than that! Paul later said, "The wife is bound by the law as long as her husband liveth; but if her husband be dead, she is at liberty to be married to whom she will, only in the Lord" (1 Cor. 7:39).

But someone asks, "Suppose there *is* a separation, in spite of the teaching of the Word of God against it?" The Apostle's next sentence indicated that he was talking about a situation where both parties were Christians. Suppose a Christian wife *does* depart. What is she to do? Verse 11 states, "Let her remain unmarried, or be reconciled to her husband." This applies equally to the Christian husband who, though contrary to the teaching of the Word, departs. He is to remain unmarried, or be reconciled to his wife.

God made no provision for divorce. It was allowed in Israel by Moses' decree because of the hardness of their hearts (see Matt. 19:7-8). The oft-repeated phrase in Christian circles, "The only biblical grounds for divorce is adultery" is without scriptural foundation. The Church of Jesus Christ needs to return once again to the clear teaching of her Lord on this vital matter. Let me say sincerely that there is no desire in these comments to hurt anyone who has been through the soul-shattering experience of separation, divorce, and accompanying matters *before* salvation. God has put our former lives under the blood. When you came to Christ in childlike faith, receiving Him as Saviour, God forgave and forgot. But my desire is that this study will be a warning, so that no Christian will step out of God's will and sin against the light of the Word of God!

A Mixed Situation (7:12-13)

Another difficult situation existed in Corinth, introduced by the words, "But to the rest speak I, not the Lord" (v. 12). What did the apostle mean? Was he indicating that this instruction is his own idea and not particularly the Lord's commandment? As noted previously, Christ had already spoken on the matter of divorce and remarriage. Paul was simply repeating what our Lord had already taught (vv. 10-11). But the Apostle went on to mention a situation not previously covered specifically by our Lord's words. The editors of the notes in the New Scofield Reference Bible point out, however, that Paul's statements are inspired, even though he implied otherwise. They make this comment: "Instead of disclaiming inspiration for what he writes in verse 12, the apostle is actually claiming for his own words here the same authority as for the words of Christ Himself." Therefore, under inspiration of the Holy Spirit, Paul is speaking with the authority of God on this additional problem.

In Corinth some wives had been saved but their husbands were still unconverted. Remember, Paul was talking to those who had just emerged from pagan darkness. The problem was not unlike that which many missionaries face today. The light of the Gospel had penetrated the darkness, and God in His grace had saved a husband or a wife. But the marriage partner was still an unbeliever. What a situation!

The unsaved person is often filled with hate, ridicule, or abuse. More than once in the years of my pastorate, some earnest Christian brother has come to pour out the anguish of his soul about a wife who has refused to accept the Saviour. In the typical situation the husband describes the seemingly intolerable division that plagues their home since he has come to know Christ. His wife is still an unbeliever, and there is no end of difficulty. Should he divorce her? Absolutely not! If a believer is married to an unbeliever, regardless of the circumstances, God does not want that marriage broken. Here is the command: "If any brother hath a wife that believeth not, and she be pleased to dwell with him, *let him not put her away*" (1 Cor. 7:12).

Christian wives have asked, "Pastor, what am I to do? My husband is unsaved. He refuses to let me come to church. You don't know how badly I'm treated, even the downright cruelty that I am going through. I think I should leave my husband." What does the Word of God say? Here it is: "And the woman who hath an husband that believeth not, and if he be pleased to dwell with her, *let her not leave him*" (1 Cor. 7:13). The member of the union who is a believer is responsible to do everything possible to hold the marriage together.

The Word of God forbids a Christian to marry one who is not a believer, for it says, "Be ye not unequally yoked together with unbelievers" (2 Cor. 6:14). Amos the prophet asks, "Can two walk together, except they be agreed?" (Amos 3:3) Perhaps someone reading this has already disobeyed this command and the marriage has been consummated. What should the believing mate do? No question about this: the believer is *not* to leave his or her partner.

The "Why" of This Command (7:14)

The marriage is to be held intact for a definite reason: "For the unbelieving husband is sanctified by the wife, and the unbelieving wife is sanctified by the husband" (1 Cor. 7:14). This is a difficult verse indeed. The interpretation depends upon the meaning of the word *sanctify*. This term is used in various ways in the Scriptures. In Genesis 2:3 we read that God "sanctified" the seventh day. Exodus 19:23 records that Moses was told to "sanctify" the mountain. In Isaiah 66:17 we read of a group of people who "sanctified themselves" to do evil. The word *sanctify* simply means, "to set apart."

The Apostle Paul is certainly not teaching that the unbelieving wife or husband is "made holy" by being married to a Christian. Then what does he mean? The unbelieving mate is "set apart" to a position of privilege. He or she is in a relationship with a believing mate that may ultimately lead to his or her salvation. The unbeliever in that marital union is "set apart" as the prayerful object of the believer's concern.

My father was still an unbeliever when my mother trusted Christ. Not only an unbeliever but an agnostic, my father despised the Bible and tried to persuade my mother not to attend church, nor to take my sister to Sunday School. My mother prayed for him faithfully. He was "set apart" as an object of her intercession. The very day and hour that he trusted Christ, my mother and a group of ladies were in our home praying for his conversion.

If the believing mate leaves, the opportunity to win the unbeliever is lost. Surely the circumstances can be difficult. The time may come when you think you cannot possibly go on another day. But if you leave, the opportunity for Christian testimony is gone. You may forfeit the potential of seeing that unsaved husband or wife come to receive Christ.

What About the Children?
In any marriage between saved and unsaved, deep concern should be shown for the children of that union. The Apostle says, "For the unbelieving husband is sanctified by the wife, and the unbelieving wife is sanctified by the husband; else were your

children unclean, but now are they holy" (1 Cor. 7:14). The same word formerly translated "sanctified" is used and here translated "holy." For clarity, it should be translated in both instances "set apart." Children in the marriage of a Christian and unbeliever are in the place of privilege as long as either mate does not put away the other.

"But," says some Christian wife, "it would be better for me to leave and take the children with me, than to let them remain under the unwholesome influence of my unbelieving husband." First of all, that would be in violation of what Paul has already said, "Let her not leave him." But if the believing wife should leave and have custody of the children, the opportunity to win them for Christ is lessened. For, if what the believer professes to have as a Christian is not able to see him or her through this difficult situation, then the children will doubt its reality. Or, if the children should go with the unbelieving mate, the believer's influence will be lost entirely.

Christian, if you are married to an unbeliever and the circumstances are difficult and trying, ask God to give you the grace to "stay with it." By remaining in obedience to the Word of God, you put yourself on ground where the Lord can do something for you. To do otherwise is disobedience. Your leaving jeopardizes the possibility of others being saved. "For what knowest thou, O wife, whether thou shalt save thy husband? Or what knowest thou, O man, whether thou shalt save thy wife?" (1 Cor. 7:16)

If the Unbeliever Departs (7:15)

The Apostle Paul continues his Spirit-inspired instructions to Christians involved in mixed marriage by saying, "But if the unbelieving depart, let him depart. A brother or a sister is not under bondage in such cases; but God hath called us to peace" (1 Cor. 7:15). Already he has clearly stated that the believer is never to seek a separation. But this is another case. If the unbeliever leaves, the believer is not to blame for that action, nor is he or she under bondage in such cases. To try and stop the unbelieving mate would probably bring further disorder to the home. But Paul said, "God hath called us to peace."

This verse does not mean that the Christian is now free to remarry if the unsaved mate departs. This would be a violation of the Word of God and surely bring chastisement (see again v. 39). To the Romans the Apostle gave additional evidence. Although illustrating a spiritual truth about the law, the fact stated remains indisputable. "For the woman who hath a husband is bound by the law to her husband as long as he liveth; but if the husband be dead, she is loosed from the law of her husband. So, then if, while her husband liveth, she be married to another man, she shall be called an adulteress; but if her husband be dead, she is free from that law, so that she is no adulteress, though she be married to another man" (Rom. 7:2-3).

Once a marriage union is entered into, there can be no other true marriage during the lifetime of the parties living. The principle of Romans 7 is restated in 1 Corinthians 7, and directly applies to our situation today.

This passage teaches that if a separation must occur between a believer and an unbeliever, the unbeliever must initiate that action. The Christian husband or wife is never to leave the unsaved mate.

Conclusion

Do you not sense within the church today a precarious inclination to minimize or reinterpret the standards of the Word of God when those standards get in the way of present-day practice? Doesn't this explain much of the current moral decay within our society? We must never forget it— God leaves no loopholes for sin! Theodore Epp, in his excellent booklet entitled *Marriage and Divorce,* says,

"Jesus gave neither His disciples nor the Pharisees permission for divorce. He reiterated the foundation principle as it was given in the beginning without amending it or adding to it. God permitted divorce during the time of the law. But it was permitted to those in Israel who were uncircumcised at heart. They were circumcised in flesh but not in heart; they were backslidden. That which was permitted for the uncircumcised in heart in Israel should not serve as a rule for those in whom the love of God has operated through the Holy Spirit."

May the Apostle's words to the church in Corinth ring forth loud and clear to the Church today!

6

Limitations of Christian Liberty

(1 Corinthians 8:1-13)

The Bible is remarkably up to date! It speaks directly to the subtle temptations and complex moral problems of our 20th-century world, giving us much-needed direction in the difficult "gray areas." So, even though the Christian today is not faced with the specific problem dealt with in this passage —eating meats sacrificed to idols—he is called upon repeatedly to apply the principles set forth in 1 Corinthians 8:11. The meaning and extent of Christian liberty must be considered by all who are loyal to the Word of God and committed to obey it. In this chapter, as in Romans 14 and 15, we have clear instruction and admonition concerning Christian liberty and how we use it.

Serious discussion, perhaps even divisions, had arisen in the Corinthian church concerning meat that had been offered to idols. Corinth was a pagan city, and Christians were living in the midst of its degraded system of religious practices which included animal sacrifices. The meat that the priests did not eat was sold to the public in the marketplace, and certain choice portions were kept by the one making the offering, to be used on the table at home.

These practices forced the believers of Corinth to face several perplexing questions. First, should Christians buy meat which had been offered to pagan idols? Second, should a believer visiting in a heathen home eat this meat? Some of the Corinthian Christians had no scruples about eating it, but others did. The Apostle Paul was apprised of the situation, and through inspiration of the Holy Spirit he set down for Corinthian believers some guidelines.

Twentieth-century believers are not confronted with this exact problem, but principles for Christian behavior related to eating meat can be applied to many other moral questions today, such as amusements, pleasures, questionable business ventures, how to spend the Lord's day, the holding of stocks in certain corporations, and scores of other difficult issues.

Knowledge Versus Love (vv. 1-3)

After mentioning the problem, Paul clearly answers it for himself and all other strong Christians. He says, "We know that we all have knowledge." Another translation renders this, "We all know, to be sure, what is the truth about it." All who have been born again, who are "in Christ," have acquired a certain amount of knowledge about Christianity. But knowledge is a deadly thing when not controlled, motivated, and tempered with love. Paul warns, "Knowledge puffeth up, but love edifieth"

(v. 1). The conceited Christian is always trying to display his knowledge, while the one who combines it with love uses it to help someone else. The former often tears down the work of God, while the latter builds it up. The Apostle Paul wrote, "For if a man think himself to be something, when he is nothing, he deceiveth himself" (Gal. 6:3). The writer of Proverbs says, "Seest thou a man wise in his own conceit? There is more hope of a fool than of him" (Prov. 26:12). Had these Corinthian Christians tempered their knowledge with the Governor of love, the questions about eating meats would never have arisen.

Perhaps you recall hearing some Christian say, "You and I both know there is nothing wrong in that." This reasoning has often been used as the go-ahead signal for participation in all kinds of activities that are not wrong in themselves, but which might cause an immature or weak brother to stumble. In fact, some Christians seem to enjoy flaunting their disregard of conventional practices, and brag about their superior knowledge as they participate in such "harmless" activities. But their knowledge is not controlled by love, and they often do spiritual damage to someone else.

God Versus Idols (vv. 4-6)

The Apostle noted two facts that every strong Christian already knew. First, they knew that an idol is "nothing"—just a piece of wood, stone, or metal. Every intelligent, informed believer in Corinth was aware of that! Second, they knew that there is only one true God, that He is the Creator and Sustainer of all things, and that He has been revealed by Jesus Christ.

Eating meat sacrificed to idols was not a matter of serious concern to these strong Christians. They were secure in Christ. Knowing what they did, were they completely free to eat of that meat or not?

Don't forget, "knowledge puffeth up." Great care must be used as principles of Christian liberty are applied today. We are *not* free to participate in practices even when they in themselves are not necessarily injurious. Even harmless things become harmful when one becomes enslaved to them.

God's judgment came upon Israel, as recorded in Numbers 25, not only because they ate meat sacrificed to idols, but also because they had engaged in idolatry. Even the twelve apostles had forbidden the eating of such meat (Acts 15). But fuller revelation given to Paul had brought a new liberty to him and to those who heard his teaching. They knew an idol had no substance or being. Therefore, meat was not profaned if offered to an idol, and, for the stronger brother, it remained God's pure gift.

Strong Versus Weak (vv. 7-9)

But not every Christian in Corinth had a true concept of his liberty. They had been so enslaved in idol worship that it was difficult for them to grasp the whole picture. Paul carefully explained that "the things which the Gentiles sacrifice, they sacrifice to demons, and not to God" (1 Cor. 10:20). Behind all idolatrous worship stands the devil and the demon world. For these weaker Christians to eat this meat, therefore, would have defiled their consciences.

Suppose one of these weaker believers who didn't know that "the idol is nothing" were to see a fellow Christian sitting in a heathen temple eating meat that had been sacrificed to images of false gods. He would consider doing it also, being made bold by the example, but he would be acting against the dictates of his conscience. Of course, as Paul stated, it would make no difference to the strong Christian whether he ate the meat or not. But just because he is not affected by it, and his conscience is not being defiled, is he free to do so?

The overriding principle of Christian love in action is stated in verse 9: "But take heed lest by any means this liberty of yours become a stumbling block to them that are weak." This guideline is to govern all believers, especially the instructed ones. Christian liberty must *not* be abused. Paul emphasized this when he wrote, "Let us not, therefore, judge one another any more; but judge this, rather: that no man put a stumbling block or an occasion to fall in his brother's way. I know, and am persuaded by the Lord Jesus, that there is nothing unclean of itself; but to him that esteemeth anything to be unclean, to him it is unclean. But if thy brother be grieved with thy food, now walkest thou not in love. Destroy not him with thy food, for whom Christ died" (Rom. 14:13-15).

Believers are given two main responsibilities in these verses. First, we are not to judge one another. The stronger brother is not to condemn the weak, nor is the weaker brother to judge the strong. Second, from the phrase "judge this, rather," we learn that we must be certain that we are not "stumbling blocks." Peter further emphasized this when he wrote, "As free, and not using your liberty for a cloak of maliciousness, but as the servants of God" (1 Peter 2:16). The Apostle Paul also admonished, "For, brethren, ye have been called unto liberty; only use not liberty for an occasion to the flesh, but *by love serve one another*" (Gal. 5:13).

What will it be? As a Christian instructed in the Word, what is your choice? A service of love or a stumbling block? (To tempt weak and ignorant Christians, or those young in the faith, is a terrible transgression; to cause them to fall is even worse.) The question that should always be asked is not primarily, "Will this harm me?" but rather, "Will this harm my weaker brother?")

Important Influence (vv. 10-11)

(Someone is always watching you. If you doubt that, just stumble and fall on the street and see how many people seemingly come from nowhere and congregate around you. Paul said, "If any man see thee." This fact is adequate reason for the Christian to take heed unto himself and to the doctrine (see 1 Tim. 4:16). Make sure of this, believer, you are being observed by other Christians.)

The Apostle illustrated with a hypothetical situation in which a Christian is eating a meal in a pagan temple. He knows he is secure in Christ, so his conscience is not affected. But a weaker brother passes the idol's temple and sees his fellow believer eating meat that had been offered to idols. What effect would it have upon him? The Apostle implied extreme consequences when he asked, "And through thy knowledge shall the weak brother perish, for whom Christ died?" The word *perish* means to be "destroyed" or "marred." Paul is not talking about a true believer being lost, but about one whose Christian life would be hindered or perhaps ruined as a result of seeing his brother eating in the heathen temple. Christian love should cause us to consider the results of the use of our liberty. The most important consideration, then, is, "Will this harm my brother?" If another Christian's spirituality might be jeopardized by our action, then in love we must abstain from doing it. The Apostle says later, "Let no man seek his own, but every man another's wealth" (1 Cor. 10:24). Our liberty is therefore limited by our love for our fellow believer.

Effect upon the Strong (v. 12)

Not only is the weaker brother harmed when we exercise a liberty uncontrolled by love, there is also a commensurate effect upon the one who harmed him. Paul said, "Ye sin against Christ." That weak brother is a member of the body of which Christ is the head. "And whether one member suffer, all the members suffer with it" (1 Cor. 12:26). Paul learned this lesson on the road to Damascus. He was determined to bring followers of Christ back to Jerusalem in chains. The Bible tells us he was "breathing out threatenings and slaughter against the disciples of the Lord" (Acts 9:1). All the hatred of his heart was directed against Christians. But then, confronted by a light from heaven, he fell to the ground and heard the voice of the risen Christ say to him, "Saul, Saul, why persecutest thou *Me?*" (Acts 9:4) What a revelation! His despicable treatment of the believers was in reality directed against Christ Himself. Ever after that, Paul was careful not to "wound Christ" by doing harm to a fellow believer. The Saviour and His saints are one. An intimate union exists between the weakest of Christ's own and Himself. Any blow that strikes one of them touches Him.

We do well, therefore, to remember the double-pronged effect of liberty uncontrolled by love. First, the indulgence of self mars the spirit of the weaker Christian brother; and second, it is a sin against Christ. Since Christ died for this brother, is it too much to ask that we limit our liberty for him?

Conclusion (v. 13)

Paul has been carefully analyzing the whole matter of the strong and weak Christian on what we call "doubtful things." How different the attitude of the Apostle Paul from that so often expressed by "strong" Christians! His was no brash display of liberty; no proud flexing of spiritual muscles to demonstrate that "it doesn't hurt me." The Apostle could eat meat in a pagan temple because he knew that idols were nothing. Nevertheless he would not do so, lest his indulgence could cause spiritual harm to his brother for whom Christ had given His very life. (You may be sure that God will guard His "weak" child. But this in no way minimizes the transgression of the believer who leads his brother to sin against his conscience.)

The grace of God expressed in the life of the believer will encourage the exercise of liberty in love. We should hear the Apostle and follow his example, "Wherefore, if food make my brother to offend, I will eat no meat while the world standeth, lest I make my brother to offend" (1 Cor. 8:13). If all Christians practiced this today, what blessing, what growth, what unity of purpose, what power would be in the church! Devotion to the Lord Jesus and love for our brethren does limit our liberty, but it in turn strengthens both our fellow believers and ourselves.

Even now, we have much to gain in spiritual experience by promoting the growth of other Christians. To be absolutely sure that our influence registers on the positive side, we must take periodic "readings" of our practices, habits, associations, and activities. Remember, "love edifieth." We prove that we love our brethren to the extent that we forego some harmless pursuit to avoid wounding his conscience. Simply to plead, "There's no harm in that, for it does not hurt me," suggests that ego has been inflated by knowledge. To desire the good of our brother is to demonstrate both our love for him and our appreciation for Christ, who died for both of us. Love-controlled liberty truly honors our Lord

7

Relinquishing Our Rights

1 Corinthians 9

The Apostle Paul had taught the Word in Corinth for 18 months (Acts 18:11). If you had visited him in the home of Aquila at that time, you would have found him at work, the same as those to whom he ministered. During the week he made tents, a trade he had learned in his youth, to support himself financially. He labored at his craft so that he might "make the Gospel of Christ without charge" (1 Cor. 9:18), and to avoid becoming a burden to the believers in Corinth.

Paul was putting into practice the important principle for Christian living which is stated in 1 Corinthians 6:12: "All things are lawful unto me, but all things are not expedient; all things are lawful for me, but I will not be brought under the power of any." He would repeat the same concept later (1 Cor. 10:23), and he devoted this large portion of his letter to explain the nature of his ministry.

We live today in a "rights-oriented" society. Ethnic groups, students, unions, women, teachers—all are demanding their rights. Some are legitimate demands; perhaps others are not. The spirit of the age often surfaces within the church, and we must confront the same issues as those being battled about in the world. Swept up with the times, we so quickly forget what is expressed by the Apostle in verse 17, as translated by W. J. Conybeare, "I am a slave entrusted with a stewardship" (*The Life and Epistles of Saint Paul*, W. J. Conybeare and J. S. Howson).

The question of rights had arisen in the Corinthian church in relation to Paul. Some believers evidently felt that he had not been using the rights that were his, both by nature as a man and by Scripture as an apostle. There were a few, in fact, who were openly questioning his authority. This section of the letter was written to reassert his apostleship and to clarify the entire question of the rights of a Christian.

Paul's Claim to Apostleship (vv. 1-3)

In dealing with his own delicate situation, Paul described himself as one who was being charged or accused of a wrong. He addressed his answer "to them that do examine me" (v. 3). Literally, Paul was saying that this is "my defense to them that examine me."

The Judaizers no doubt had said, "This Paul, he's no apostle! If he were, he would be using the rights of an apostle." Some scholars believe that Christians were always a little suspicious of Paul in Jerusalem after his conversion. This distrust probably carried over to Corinth, and may have appeared in other locations. Paul had once before defended his apostleship in his letter to the church in Galatia. To them he claimed direct revelation from Jesus Christ and no conference with men in receiving the doctrine he preached. "I conferred not with flesh and blood; neither went I up to Jerusalem to them who were apostles before me" (Gal. 1:16-17).

Note the questions he asked of the Corinthians: "Am I not free? Have I not seen Jesus Christ, our Lord? Are not ye my work in the Lord?" (v. 1) Someone apparently had been saying to Paul, "You're no apostle. You didn't see the Lord, and you weren't with Him in His earthly ministry following His resurrection." They had forgotten that apostles were chosen directly by the Lord Jesus. Peter himself had neglected this on one occasion. Dr. M. R. De Haan said in his book *Pentecost and After,* "Peter, unable in his impatience to wait for instructions from the Lord at Pentecost, suggests they hold an election. . . . Peter was completely out of order, for they had been commanded to *wait* for the Holy Spirit to direct them. . . . Instead of waiting for the divine appointment of God's ordained apostle (Paul), they set up a slate of candidates and cast lots to see who would win."

(Paul got his authority for apostleship when he personally met with the risen Christ. He said, "And last of all He was *seen of me also,* as of one born out of due time")(1 Cor. 15:8). The record of that tremendous experience is in Acts 9, which tells us of his conversion.)The word of Christ to Ananias about Paul was, "Go thy way; for he is a chosen vessel unto Me, to bear My name before the Gentiles, and kings, and the children of Israel" (Acts

9:15). (Here indeed was a chosen apostle—one called of Christ, separated unto the ministry, sent by the Lord, and one who exercised delegated authority.

God has given His seal upon the apostleship of Paul, an insignia of his authority. The Apostle asks, "Are not *ye* my work in the Lord?" He had planted the Corinthian church; he was its master builder. The believers at Corinth were the proof of his calling. Both by appointment and visible evidence, therefore, God had given His approval of the apostleship claimed by Paul.

Paul's Rights (vv. 4-14)

As an apostle of the Lord Jesus, Paul had the same rights as his fellow disciples. He mentioned three of them in verses 4-6, as he began the defense of his authority.

1. "Have we no right to eat and to drink?" Paul was saying here that he could have secured for himself a regular supply of the necessities of life. A comfortable existence could have been assured, and it would have been his by perfect right within the church. But he chose not to have it.

2. "Have we no right to lead about a sister, a wife, as well as other apostles, and as the brethren of the Lord, and Cephas?" He also had every right to enjoy the pleasures of domestic life if he so decided. But he was willing to forego them that he might fulfill his calling as the apostle of the Gentiles.

3. "Or I only, and Barnabas, have we no right to forbear working?" Those who labored so hard in the interest of the souls of men surely had every right to be spared from the additional weariness

of physical toil. But Paul labored anyway, for the sake of the Christian's.

As an apostle, Paul had the right to have his needs supplied, to enjoy family life, and to have freedom from physical toil. But in Corinth he had chosen not to avail himself of them. He had not asked the Corinthian Christians for any financial support. This hadn't been true of Paul in every place he labored. Nor with every church he visited. But it was the case at Corinth.

He underscored his right to remuneration by pointing to the example of a universal law of nature (v. 7). (No soldier carries on warfare at his own expense. The military man who surrenders his life for the defense of his country is entitled in turn to his government's support. No one would challenge that. The farmer eats the fruit of the field which he has planted and cultivated, and no one would question his right to do so. The shepherd who keeps a flock, feeding and protecting it, has a right to drink the milk of that flock. Who would argue with that?)

But the affirmation of nature is not the only basis for claiming the rights, for the Old Testament teaches it as well. Paul reminded these Corinthians that the law of Moses prohibited the muzzling of an ox as it treads out the grain, so that it may eat and be nourished. Furthermore, the priests who ministered before God were sustained by portions of that which they offered in the temple.

No question about it! "Even so hath the Lord ordained that they who preach the Gospel should live of the Gospel" (v. 14). It is a divine principle that churches are responsible to provide for the temporal needs of those who minister to them in spiritual things. For believers to "sow sparingly" in this phase of the testimony of the church will without doubt bring about a meager reaping. We may call it "paying the preacher," but in reality it is obedience to a divine principle.

Paul's Response to His Rights (vv. 15-23)

That which was a matter of self-interest and privilege became an opportunity for self-sacrifice on behalf of Christ and His Gospel. Paul said, "But I have used none of these things" (v. 15). He had given up the right to claim sustenance, the right to enjoy the pleasures of domestic life, and the right to forego physical labor in secular employment, for the Gospel's sake.

There were times when Paul had accepted remuneration, though not at Corinth. The Apostle mentioned gifts he had received from other churches (2 Cor. 11:8), but not from the Corinthians, lest in their case he should hinder the Gospel of Christ. The same principle as shown in chapter 6 has additional relevance in this one: knowledge must be tempered with love. Paul held his own rights in check (and he had knowledge of those rights) by the constraining love of Christ within him. His love for the souls of men, as well as for the Gospel he preached, caused him to refrain from demanding those things which were rightfully his as an apostle.

The Rights of a Slave

The apostle used a striking phrase here: "For necessity is laid upon me" (v. 16). The word "necessity" refers to the compulsion exercised by a master over a slave. Paraphrasing this verse, Conybeare renders it, "For, although I claim the glad tidings, yet this gives me no ground of boasting; *for I am compelled to do so by order of my Master"* *(The Life and Epistles of Saint Paul).* Really now, what rights has a slave? He has the right to obey his master. He has the right to be well-pleasing to the one who owns him. All other rights are forfeited so that he may give undivided attention and complete obedience to the will of his master.

The fact that Paul was a bond slave to Jesus Christ enabled him to be a "servant unto all, that I might gain the more" (v. 19). I have a friend who preaches a sermon entitled, "The Order of the Towel," in reference to the cloth used by the Lord Jesus when He washed the disciples' feet. He suggests that Christian churches ought to have towels on their steeples, in keeping with Jesus' statement, "He that humbleth himself shall be exalted" (Luke 14:11). Like the Master, in John 13, we are to take the place of a servant.

Church quarrels would quickly come to an end, and bitter disputes for position would have no fuel for the fire if Christians, like the apostle, would become "servant unto all." Our Lord's example should be impressed deeply upon our hearts and followed in every situation.

Dr. H. A. Ironside, the well-known Bible commentator, recalled an incident in his boyhood when some highly respected churchmen became angry with one another. He was shocked as he watched the scene. One man, springing to his feet and clenching his fist, shouted, "I will not allow you to put anything over on me; I will have my rights!"

An old Scotsman, rather hard of hearing, leaned forward and cupped his ear with his hand so he would not miss any of the proceedings. "What was that, brother?" he asked, "I didn't quite get your point."

"I said, I will have my rights!" retorted the man.

"But surely you did not mean that, did you?" came the reply. "If you insisted on what was coming to you, you would be in Hell. Jesus did not come to get His rights; He came to get our wrongs, and He got them!"

The wise old gentleman's words struck home. For a moment the indignant protester stood there, and then tears broke from his eyes. "Brethren," he said sorrowfully, "I have been all wrong. Handle the case as you think best." Then he sat down with his face in his hands and sobbed repentantly.

Paul's Humility of Spirit

What power accompanied the Apostle's preaching! His style and method of proclaiming the Gospel demonstrated an attitude of submission and servitude. He renounced his personal and apostolic rights, and became "slave of all" in order to "gain the more" (v. 19). To those under the law he freely gave up his liberty that he might reach them. To those without law (the Gentiles) he became as a Gentile in order to win them. But never once did he compromise the Gospel. He gave up his own rights willingly and became a love slave. Then he said, "And this I do for the Gospel's sake" (v. 23).

He had done even more than support himself by the labor of his own hands, for he had accommodated himself to every situation. The conclusion, shown in verse 22, is always a good rule for the Christian to follow: "I am made all things to all men, that I might by all means save some."

What About Our Rights?

Tragically, the same sad comment the Apostle made of some in Philippi would have to be said of us: "For all seek their own, not the things which are Jesus Christ's" (Phil. 2:21). We do have rights. But will those rights be used for self-interest, or will they become an opportunity for self-sacrifice? What transformation of life and ministry ought to be evident in every believer! It could be, if with love for Christ and our brethren we would relinquish our rights and become true bond slaves of Jesus Christ.

Rights in the Church

We acknowledge that God has established a certain order in the local church. He is not only the God of grace but also the God of government. The distinct command in Hebrews must be followed: "Remember them [your church leaders] who have the rule over you, who have spoken unto you the word of God, whose faith follow, considering the end of their manner of life" (Heb. 13:7). The risen Christ has set some in the church in positions of authority and responsibility. The pastor is both an undershepherd and an overseer. Deacons and elders, chosen of God, have unique responsibilities within the assembly.

Many of the difficulties and problems confronting local churches do not stem from a disregard of God's appointed order, but from an unwillingness of believers to forego their "rights" for the good of the Body of Christ and the sake of the Gospel. Consider the following questions:

1. Though I am older and more experienced, would I

be willing to relinquish my Sunday School class to a younger Christian so that he can exercise his gift?

2. I have been a church officer for a long time. It is expected that since I have functioned in this position for a number of years, I will continue to be elected. Am I willing, joyfully so, to step aside and give another the opportunity of service?

3. I have served faithfully, giving of my time, effort, and money in the work of the church. Strange to say, no one has expressed appreciation. Would I continue this service if I knew no word of praise or appreciation would ever be given me?

There are other rights which may be yours as a Christian, united with other believers in a local church. They may include rights as one who is gifted in public ministry; or perhaps rights which are yours because of position, length of service, standing in the community, or abilities peculiarly yours by God's grace. List on a piece of paper these rights. Then check off those you would be willing to relinquish for Christ, His Church, other believers, and the Gospel.

What peace would reign in the Church if we followed the example of the Apostle! His relationship with the Corinthian believers and his command: "Be kindly affectioned one to another with brotherly love, *in honor preferring one another*" (Rom. 12:10), set the pattern for every believer. Though we are Christ's free men, we are privileged to "gain the more" by making ourselves servants unto all. The rights of the servant are subjugated to the will of Christ, the Master.

8

Temptation and Triumph

1 Corinthians 10:1-13

The pictures in a family album tell some interesting stories. Most of them are pleasant. Some bring happy memories, but others cause us to relive experiences barbed with lessons learned and predicaments to be avoided. I recall one snapshot in my parent's collection that showed a freshly painted side of our house with smeared handmarks leading to a ladder that had fallen to the ground. That picture, though with humorous connotations, reminds us of a specific lesson that was learned the hard way: a ladder perched precariously on something less than a solid foundation will end in spilled paint and shaken painter. Yes, that old picture album is quite articulate!

This is exactly what we have in 1 Corinthians 10—the Apostle Paul pulled out the picture album. Thoroughly familiar with the history of his nation, Israel, he drew, with Spirit-inspired pen, from that chronicle a number of experiences which would be

84

beneficial to both the Corinthians and 20th-century believers. He said, in fact, "Now all these things happened unto them *for examples,* and they are written *for our admonition*" (1 Cor 10:11). The history of the Old Testament is to be used not only for application but also for our profit and learning. Think of it! In God's dealing with His ancient people Israel, we have a picture album with the divine notation on each experience: "This is for your training." "All Scripture is profitable." No experience in the lives of the children of Israel was superfluous. God wasted no copy in relating their history in His Word. So let's open the picture album!

This passage begins with the word "moreover," which is literally translated, "for." The Apostle was connecting what he had to say about Israel with the preceding subject. When he mentioned the possibility of becoming a "castaway," or "disapproved" (1 Cor. 9:27), he was speaking of service, *not* salvation. In chapter 10 he was illustrating what he meant, giving examples of Israel in the exodus. Of all who left Egypt, only two who were more than 20 years of age were allowed to enter the promised land (Num. 14:29-31). Idolatry, lust, murmuring, and unbelief had kept the others from the land "flowing with milk and honey." They had succumbed to temptation, even though God had provided adequately for their success. He had promised them the land. It was theirs. All they had to do was possess it. The same is assured to us. The Apostle Paul was continuing a theme he had stated previously, "So, run, that ye may obtain" (1 Cor. 9:24).

Believers are to live so that they will gain the prize and have the Judge's commendation. This goal was constantly in Paul's own mind as he labored for the Lord. Like Israel, he had been delivered—redeemed. He did not want to be disapproved. He wanted to run the race and engage in the conflict so that he might face his Lord in triumph. No fear that he would ever be lost lurked in his heart. He could say with confidence, "I know whom I have believed and am persuaded that He is able to keep that which I have committed unto Him against that day" (2 Tim. 1:12).

In chapter 9, Paul clearly stated the privileges and rights of his apostleship. Yet he could see the possibility of falling short of that which God had provided for him. He knew that privilege offers no guarantee against failure. Any Christian could succumb to temptation and go down in defeat—saved, yet stripped of reward.

Israel's Privilege (vv. 1-4)

Look at the picture album and see the place of favor Israel enjoyed. Her redemption from Egypt is an object lesson of the believer's deliverance from sin. The inspired record lists the privileges of this redeemed nation:

1. "All our fathers were under the cloud." When the children of Israel reached the Red Sea, the glory cloud appeared to direct them. As they made their way through the desert, they were divinely led and protected. The psalmist David said, "He spread a cloud for a covering, and fire to give light in the night" (Ps. 105:39).

2. "All passed through the sea." For Israel, crossing the sea meant deliverance. They were brought out of the land of Egypt and emancipated from bondage. In that cloud and sea they were delivered from

all the conditions of slavery to the Egyptians. The Lord Himself had become their Saviour-God!

3. "Were all baptized unto Moses." Just as believers are baptized to symbolize their identification with Christ, so the Israelites were set apart in union with Moses, the deliverer appointed by God.

4. "Did all eat the same spiritual food." This refers to those years in the wilderness when Israel ate the manna, demonstrating that God had not abandoned them after deliverance from Egypt. Manna was the provision made for their sustenance and keeping. Once in the desert they could not provide food for themselves, so it came directly from God.

5. "Did all drink the same spiritual drink." Moses smote a rock at Horeb, and they were given an abundant supply of water (Exodus 17:1-6). Like the manna, this was not a natural provision but a miraculous supply.

Note again the privileges of Israel: deliverance, guidance, protection, identification, and sustenance. It was all of God; nothing of themselves. What a wonderful privilege was theirs! Writing to the Corinthians, Paul must have sensed what their reaction to this Old Testament account would be. Certainly a people so privileged would walk in obedience to the God who had delivered them. What a powerful impression these events should have had upon Israel!

Divine Displeasure (v. 5)

It is dangerous to enjoy the blessings of God's providence yet presume upon His grace. Note what happened to the Israelites. "But with many of them God was not well pleased; for they were overthrown in the wilderness" (1 Cor. 10:5). A more accurate translation would be, "But with *most* of them." In fact, of the people who came out of Egypt, all except Caleb and Joshua perished in the wilderness.

Because these things were our examples, we do well to extract the practical value of this Old Testament teaching. Keep in mind that Canaan was *not* an object lesson of heaven, but stood for the believer's present blessings as he walks in faith. Egypt represented the world, the wilderness, the flesh; the conflicts in Canaan were the satanic principalities and powers against which the believer wrestles (Eph. 6:12-18).

The Apostle Paul mentioned five sins which are stern warnings to every believer (1 Cor. 10:6-10). We may say, "We are Christians, so it doesn't matter how we live." We may glory in all of our privileges, but this does not ensure us against failure. The five "alls" in verses 1 through 4 emphasize the five downward steps of the children of Israel, as stated in verses 6 through 10.

1. *Lust* (v. 6) The phrase reads literally, "They set their hearts" on forbidden things. Moses wrote, "And the mixed multitude that was among them fell to lusting, and the children of Israel also wept again, and said, 'Who shall give us flesh to eat?' " (Num. 11:4) They desired something that was not part of God's provision. The heavenly food with its original taste of "wafers made with honey" (Ex. 16:31) began to taste like "fresh oil" (Num. 11:8) when the Israelites lusted after flesh.

I have observed Christians who have grown tired of God's Word and sought some sensation or excitement that appeals to the flesh. Rather than being satisfied with the solid food and refreshing water of the Word of God, they have lusted after other delights. The psalmist, speaking of Israel, said, "He gave them their request, but sent leanness into their soul" (Ps. 106:15).

2. *Idolatry* (v. 7) The scene the Apostle Paul recalls next is probably the incident recorded in Exodus 32. Moses had gone up the mountain to receive the law. While he was away, the people gathered around Aaron and demanded that he make them gods. Aaron collected their golden jewelry and fashioned a calf, which the people worshiped. This led to an outbreak of the lust of the flesh in the camp of Israel. The account says that "the people sat down to eat and to drink, and rose up to play" (Ex. 32:6). The Levites were appointed the executioners and 3,000 were slain in judgment.

We today live in an age of materialism. The golden calves are many. We are given the warning, "For this ye know, that no fornicator, nor unclean person, nor covetous man (who is an idolator)hath any inheritance in the kingdom of Christ and of God" (Eph. 5:5). Affections set upon fleshly things can bring only the chastening hand of God. When Christ is *dethroned*, of necessity an idol is *enthroned*. The Christian must make certain that nothing is substituted in his heart for the Lord Jesus Christ.

3. *Fornication* (v. 8) Numbers 25 tells the frightful story of how the men of Israel committed adultery with the daughters of Moab. This also is "written for our admonition." The warning is certainly against physical fornication, but it extends beyond that for the believer. Speaking of spiritual adultery, James wrote, "Ye adulterers and adulteresses, know ye not that the friendship of the world is enmity with God? Whosoever, therefore,

will be a friend of the world is the enemy of God" (James 4:4).

4. *Tempting God* (v. 9) This refers to trying the patience of God, putting Him to the test, which is really a sin of unbelief. Numbers 21 gives the historical account of the event in Israel's history. How great the patience of the Lord had been with His people! They had refused His gracious provision and complained about the daily supply of manna. Their sin finally brought judgment, and many perished when God sent fiery serpents among them. Psalm 78:12-32 records how long-suffering the Lord had been with Israel, and that they still were not satisfied.

5. *Murmuring* (v. 10) Murmuring is an old expression of dissatisfaction, a sin in God's sight. We are told, "And the people spoke against God, and against Moses, 'Wherefore have ye brought us up out of Egypt to die in the wilderness? For there is no bread, neither is there any water; and our soul loatheth this light bread'" (Num. 21:5). Their murmuring reached such a degree that the people said, "Let us make a captain, and let us return to Egypt" (Num 14:4). They complained in many different ways on their wilderness journey. They murmured when God judged by destroying Korah, Dathan, and Abiram. They murmured against Moses, and this led to a worse sin. The sad account of when Aaron and Miriam envied Moses is recorded in Numbers 12. Suddenly the Lord spoke, for His anger had been kindled against them. Miriam was stricken with leprosy, which resulted in her being shut out of the camp of Israel for seven days. "And the people journeyed not till Miriam was brought in again" (Num. 12:15). Think of the loss in time

and progress for the children of Israel! Six hundred thousand people multiplied by 6 meant the staggering sum of 3,600,000 man-marching-days were lost. How bitter are the consequences of murmuring against God and His servants!

I have seen similar faultfinding in Christian households. Parents, who would never take a rifle and shoot at their pastor or some Christian worker, will sit in the family circle and become spiritual snipers at their God-appointed leaders. Then they wonder why their children are rebellious, care nothing for the things of God, and have no respect for His faithful servants.

Perhaps someone now is tempted to do the same. Let the experience of Israel become a lesson to him! This privileged people failed, and as a result they were destroyed in the wilderness. They had been saved—delivered from Egypt—but they missed the blessings of walking in obedience. They did not claim the promises God had given them. The warning of 1 Corinthians 10:12 is to us: "Wherefore, let him that thinketh he standeth take heed lest he fall."

Temptation and Triumph (v. 13)

How can a believer stand firm in a world so filled with danger and evil? What keeps him from falling? Verse 13 is a mountain peak in God's Word. The believer's responsibility is to keep trusting God, who will not permit His child to be tested beyond his strength, but will furnish the way of escape in every kind of temptation. The verse reads, "There hath no temptation taken you but such as is common to man; but God is faithful, who will not permit you to be tempted above that ye are able, but will, with the temptation, also make the way to escape, that ye may be able to bear it" (1 Cor. 10:13).

Caleb and Joshua faced the same temptations as the others of Israel, but they trusted in God and were victorious. The Scriptures are filled with examples of men who stood true to God in times of severe trial and testing. Years of experience in the Christian life do not guarantee immunity to the subtle snares of temptation. What may be avoided easily by a young Christian could be the downfall of a mature believer.

A recent news release illustrates this truth. A *United Press International* story began, "We think that we shall never see, a holocaust as devastating as a professionally removed tree." The story was about a man in Washington state who wanted to remove a 100-foot fir tree from a precarious location that threatened his house. So he employed some professional tree removers. The wisdom of his decision became doubtful, however, when those "experts" made an error. They felled the tree all right, but it fell in the wrong direction and cut his house in half. I imagine those workmen had approached the job quite confidently. Perhaps they had often accomplished similar assignments with no difficulty. But this time was different. There was some element they failed to reckon with. Experienced Christians need to "take heed." Past victories may cause complacency as we meet the present temptation or an unsuspected element may catch us unawares and cause us to slip.

"But God is faithful!" Complete reliance upon Him will bring deliverance in even the most severe times of temptation. Charles Spurgeon said, "You may be tried till you have not an ounce of strength left. Sometimes the Lord tests His people till it seems as if one more breath from Him would assuredly cause them to sink. Then it is that He puts under them the everlasting arms, and no further trial is laid upon them. This is a blessed thing, for all of you have troubles of one sort or another, and you who are the people of God may take this text and rely implicitly upon it: 'God is faithful, who will not suffer you to be tempted above that ye are able.'"

Not only does God put a limit, a boundary, upon the temptation, but He also makes a way of escape. If we become too self-confident, we should not be surprised to find that the very least temptation exceeds our ability to withstand. But if the heart condition is right, and we are in utter dependence upon Him, the temptation will not be too strong for us. He will provide deliverance, so that we are able to bear it without falling.

Because of Israel's sins of lust, idolatry, fornication, tempting God, and murmuring, there was a lapse in their progress. This is graphically recorded in Hebrews 11, for between verses 29 and 30 is a period of 40 years of history. You read, "By faith they passed through the Red Sea" and the account continues, "By faith the walls of Jericho fell down." Those words may read smoothly, with no transition between the verses, but there is no "by faith" recorded for the intervening 40 years. They were at a standstill because of their sin. The pictures of that period are a sad and ugly segment in the photo album.

Not one of us needs to stumble around in a wilderness, wandering, pursuing the desires of the flesh, doubting God, or giving in to temptation. With complete confidence in the faithfulness of God, we can enter into the full riches of grace that are ours in Christ Jesus. "Blessed be the God and Father of our Lord Jesus Christ, who hath blessed us with all spiritual blessings in heavenly places in Christ" (Eph. 1:3).

Christian friend, yours is *not* an uncommon temptation. Yours *is* the God who is faithful.

9

Observing God's Order

1 Corinthians 11:1 16

At a 1975 business meeting of the first national gathering of the Evangelical Women's Caucus, participants voted to send a telegram "reaffirming solidarity with the Catholic sisters in the struggle for ordination. A resolution supporting the Equal Rights Amendment was passed with 18 opposing votes." Previously, the ecclesiastical leaders of the Anglican Church of Canada had voted to give individual bishops power to admit qualified women to the priesthood. Then a dissenting minority of the clergy in that church issued a manifesto stating, "It is an impossibility in the divine economy for a woman to be a priest."

The probability of 1 Corinthians 11:1-16 ever being adopted by the modern feminist movement as the words for its theme song is rather remote. It is also doubtful that the use of a veil in Bible times could be equated with women wearing hats in church today. As there comes an increasing demand

95

for the ordination of women within Protestant circles, we must ask what the Bible says about "equal rights" within the church. If your blood pressure is already elevated to see if I disagree with or support your personal position, I suggest that you "cool it" until we have examined what 1 Corinthians 11:1-16 has to say.

Paul began this section, written in response to information he had received from Corinth, with a word of praise for the people of that assembly of believers. In spite of all their shortcomings, he gave credit where credit was due. He had urged them to imitate him in their Christian walk, saying, "Be ye followers of me, even as I also am of Christ" (1 Cor. 11:1), and then he commended them in the areas where they had been obedient. We would do well to follow the Apostle's example. A word of encouragement, a note of praise is always in order among God's people.

The Setting

The Christians at Corinth were relatively new believers. Both men and women had suddenly experienced the reality mentioned in 2 Corinthians 5:17, "Old things are passed away; behold, all things are become new." Having been made spiritually alive by the new birth, they had formed new relationships and found new liberty. They had then to determine how they were to live as believers. What were their attitudes to be, and what were they to do in practical, everyday situations?

We have already considered one of these practical matters in our discussion of 1 Corinthians 7. A believing husband, recently converted, wondered whether he should continue to live with his wife, who remained an unbeliever. He asked, "Should one who is a child of God maintain such an intimate relationship with one who is still dead in trespasses and sins?" Paul settled that issue by saying, "Let him not put her away" (1 Cor. 7:12). This is but one illustration of the multitude of problems facing these early Christians as they tried to live as God's obedient children in the midst of a corrupt, condemned world.

As new Christians, they began to realize the true value of all believers before God. They had learned with great joy that "there is neither Jew nor Greek, there is neither bond nor free, there is neither male nor female; for ye are all one in Christ Jesus" (Gal. 3:28). Salvation from God, accessible to all on equal terms, had brought every believer into a oneness with Christ and their fellow believers. The tyrannizing divisions were shattered when men and women became members of the Body of Christ.

This truth had a profound effect upon Christian women of Corinth. They realized they had been made *one* with Christ! They knew that man could be given no higher honor than they had been afforded as God's children. The women therefore wondered why they could not assume equal places of authority in the church and rightfully disregard their former customs of dress and appearance.

The General Principle (v. 3)
The Lord is not only the God of grace but also the God of government, of order, of authority. Though in sovereign grace He brings us to Himself, the same unerring, unchangeable principle of order that governs creation also applies in the church.

Paul stated the divine organizational pattern as: "The head of every man is Christ; and the head of the woman is the man; and the head of Christ is God" (1 Cor. 11:3). The word "head" simply and plainly means "government" or "authority." Christ has the place of supremacy, not only as head of the Church but also as the head of man. He is the "firstborn of all creation." And, because the Lord Jesus became man, living in perfect obedience to the Father, it can be truly said that "the head of Christ is God."

This divinely appointed order is not set aside in the places the Lord has given to man and woman respectively on the earth. "The head of the woman is the man." This is God's order for the husband and wife in the marriage. How much confusion would be avoided if this verse were taken to heart and applied!

I am not suggesting for one moment that woman is inferior to man. Nor am I setting aside the glorious truth that "there is in Christ neither male nor female." Just as Christ is the head of creation and of the Church, so is man the head of the woman. This in no way teaches inferiority of woman to man, any more than it teaches the inferiority of Christ to the Father. Christ is the eternal Son of God, co-equal with the Father in every way. He is *God!* But He humbled Himself, took the form of a servant, and was made in the likeness of man. As man, He took His place under God in perfect obedience. To minimize or to speak disparagingly of woman's responsibility to acknowledge the headship of the man would be to deprecate Christ's submission to the Father's will because the divine order is God, Christ, man, woman.

The Case in Corinth (vv. 5-6)

In the East, the woman veiled herself in modesty and subjection. Her veil expressed fidelity to her husband. In Numbers 5:18, the head of a wife suspected of adultery was uncovered, indicating that she had taken herself out from under the power and government of her husband. In New Testament times, reputable women wore a veil in public. Appearing without that veil, especially in a city like Corinth, was the mark of a prostitute. Often an immoral woman was not only unveiled but also shorn or shaven. But when a woman veiled herself, she showed that of her own will she accepted that subjection to her husband which nature taught her by adorning her with long hair.

The Christian women in Corinth were no doubt saying in effect, "All things are lawful to us as believers, so we don't need to wear veils." And Paul seemed to be answering, "That's true, but you are in Corinth, and to appear unveiled would be to dishonor your husband."

The dishonor does not stop there, for the man "is the image and glory of God; but the woman is the glory of man" (Cor. 11:7). Everything that violates God's order is dishonoring. The Lord has clothed woman with glory and splendor in her God-given position. And she is the glory of the man. For her to disregard, deny, or despise this authority and divine order is to dishonor herself, her husband and her Lord. Any violation of this order always brings havoc to the home, to the church, or to God's creation.

Let's not forget that the ungodly conditions of Corinth are in view here. Now that they knew God's order, these Christian women were to respect the divinely appointed authority of their husbands. Otherwise the corruption of the society that surrounded them might cause them to become disobedient.

The Expected Question

When we seek to apply this truth to our church today, a question arises immediately. Does this Scripture require women to wear hats in church? Are their heads to be adorned in public worship? I rather expect that my answer will please some and displease others. I don't want to do either, but my intention is to present clearly the principle set forth in this passage of Scripture.

C. I. Scofield said, "Nothing could be more contrary to the whole spirit of this dispensation than to use the casual mention of an ancient custom in a Greek city as fastening a legal and, so to speak, Levitical ceremony upon Christians in all ages. The point is that 'the head of the woman is the man.' It is the divine order. The angels know this. In Corinth a shorn or uncovered head in the presence of men was a badge of harlotry—of a woman who has thrown off the restraints of subordination of the divine order."

I doubt seriously that the covering of the head in the Corinth situation can be equated with women wearing hats today in the public services of the church. However, the hair and dress of a believing woman should testify to her moral character, her willing submission to her husband, and her devotion to Christ. Paul further commanded, "In like manner, also, that women adorn themselves in modest apparel, with godly fear and sobriety, not with braided hair, or gold, or pearls, or costly array, but (which becometh women professing godliness) with good works" (1 Tim 2:9-10).

I have been privileged to minister in assemblies of believers where Christian women wear a hat or lace covering on their heads. In other churches where I have fellowshiped and ministered, this practice was not followed. I observed equally godly women in both groups. They were modestly adorned, demonstrating that biblical submission which brings honor to the husband and to Christ. I would be less than candid, however, if I failed to report that I have met Christian women, both among those who wear the hat and those who do not, that were *not* obeying God's order. Whether they wore hats or not made no difference.

Someone is Looking (vv. 9-10)

The divine order, which can be observed in the scheme of redemption (vv. 3-5), in nature itself (vv. 14-15), in moral standards (vv. 6-9), and even in man's intuitive judgment (v. 13), is also the object of angels' interest. "For this cause ought the woman to have authority on her head because of the angels" (1 Cor. 11:10). This is a difficult verse to explain. The Bible tells us that angels, who are ministering spirits to the heirs of salvation, are present throughout the earth. They desire to see the order of God in the original creation carefully preserved in the church. Angels, who veil themselves in the presence of Jehovah to show their submission, would surely expect those who are redeemed by the blood of Christ to demonstrate a subordination to God's arrangement of authority. We are told in Ephesians 3:10 that by the Church will the principalities and powers in heavenly places (angels) know the manifold wisdom of God. Angels are spectators of the assembly of believers. They certainly could not abide the disarrangement of God's order. By their own example (Isa. 6:1-3), they condemn the Church when it does not recognize and submit to God's line of authority.

Paul Was No Anti-Feminist

J. Sidlow Baxter, in his interpretation of this portion of Scripture, clearly points out that Paul was not anti-feminist in his instructions. Baxter said, "His handling of the husband's headship in chapter 11 is as masterly as it is commonly misunderstood. He does not teach that the man is head of the woman but that the husband is head of the wife—for that is what is meant by the words 'man' and 'woman' in verse 3. . . . All Paul's counsels in this chapter are safeguards of Christian womanhood, not prison chains!" (J. Sidlow Baxter *Explore the Book* Vol. VI, p. 115)

Christ and His Gospel have in reality elevated womanhood. When speaking of that glorious relationship of Christ and His Church, the Apostle uses the human relationship of husband and wife (Eph. 5:22-33). No deprecator of woman was the Apostle Paul! His plea, and ours, is for the observance of the divine order, and submission is the keynote: "Submitting yourselves one to another in the fear of God" (Eph. 5:21). If this chain of authority is acknowledged in the church and in marriage, the result will be peace in the assembly and in the home, and the blessing of God will shower upon both.

10

Conduct at Communion

1 Corinthians 11:17-34

If I were to visit your home and treat a prized portrait of a departed loved one with disrespect, what would be your response? Worse yet, what if I should put a caricature or a vulgar picture in its place? This is exactly what some of the members of the church at Corinth were doing when they came together to observe an ordinance that was intended to picture the death of the Lord Jesus.

The Lord's Supper had been degraded even below the level of a common meal at Corinth. In that assembly the *agape* or "love" feast was a meal of fellowship that preceded the observance of the Lord's table. The original purpose of the love feast had been grossly perverted, as the "leaven" of the old feasts of idolatry corrupted the intended memorial. Gluttony and drunkenness had replaced devotion and spiritual refreshment. The old time Bible expositor A. T. Pierson said in a sermon published after his death, "They turned what was intended as a feast of love into a banquet of appetite, and what was intended to be a bond of fellowship into a breach of division. They desecrated the Lord's Supper; and they ate and drank judgment to themselves, 'not discerning the Lord's body.' " This ordinance, designed by our Lord to typify the most intimate of relationships, had become an occasion for partying and revelry, dishonoring the sacred picture, and the death of their Lord it represented.

Perhaps Christians today do not, in the same evil manner, dishonor the Lord at His table, but we must readily admit that there is much empty formality, presumption, and carelessness, if not outright unbelief, as we "remember Him."

The Apostle's Condemnation (vv. 17-22)
This ordinance, instituted by our Lord on the night of His betrayal, has become the center of great confusion and even heresy within the organized church today. For some, an ignorance of our Lord's purpose and design has led to a careless, indifferent spirit about its observance. For others, an unwarranted reverence for the symbols themselves—a superstitious regard of their significance —has turned the soul from personal communion with Christ, and made those simple elements to be the benefactors of grace.

The confession of faith of one of the most prominent churches in America reads, "The body and blood of Christ are truly present and are distributed to those who eat in the supper of the Lord, and we disapprove of those who teach otherwise." Another branch of Christendom believes that through the instrumentality of the priest, the substance of bread and wine become Christ's actual body and blood. The elements are said to be "consecrated," and therefore the priest, the elements, and the performance become the object of worship. Sinners are taught to look to the fruit of the vine and the bread as the means of salvation, or as they are termed, "the means of grace."

The Corinthian Christians had become careless regarding the meaning of that love feast, and were dishonoring the Lord at His table. Division had arisen over the celebration of that which should have been a unifying ordinance. Though it proclaimed that they were "one bread" and "one body," it had become a source of contention. This was an indication that they did not comprehend the true significance of the Lord's table, and the Apostle Paul condemned them. The Lord's Supper was to have been a time of communion with God and with one another. In 1 Corinthians 10 he had said, "The cup of blessing which we bless, is it not the communion of the blood of Christ? The bread which we break, is it not the communion of the body of Christ? For we being many are one bread, and one body; for we are all partakers of that one bread" (1 Cor. 10:16-17).

Communion implies joint participation. We share as partners, for we have a common bond in Christ. We sustain a common relationship to Him and derive common enjoyments from Him. If believers sit at the table of the Lord with bitterness or division between them, they deny by their very attitudes and actions that which they are observing. How dishonoring to their Lord! Anyone who finds in his heart a "root of bitterness" toward a brother or sister in Christ should not sit again at the table of the Lord until there is a reconciliation. "Therefore, if thou bring thy gift to the altar, and there remembrest that thy brother hath anything against thee, leave there thy gift before the altar, and go thy way; first be reconciled to thy brother, and then come and offer thy gift" (Matt. 5:23-24).

The Apostle Peter admonished those who have been redeemed by the precious blood of Christ: "Seeing that ye have purified your souls in obeying the truth through the Spirit unto unfeigned love of the brethren, see that ye love one another with a pure heart fervently" (1 Peter 1:22).

The Purpose of the Lord's Table (vv. 23-26)

Paul evidently received these instructions about communion by direct revelation from the Lord, for he had not been present in the upper room for the institution of the Lord's Supper. Remember, his conversion took place after the ascension of the Lord Jesus.

Because the departed Saviour knew well the tendency of man's heart to occupy itself with other things, He established these tokens to call afresh to our remembrance the scenes of Gethsemane and Calvary. The bread is to remind us of His body, which was broken for our sakes; the fruit of the vine speaks of His blood, so freely shed for our sins. The prophet said, "Yet it pleased the Lord to bruise Him; He hath put Him to grief" (Isa. 53:10). The cup contained the fruit of the vine that had been crushed, bruised, poured out.

This do," Jesus said, "in remembrance *of Me*." Paul was careful to note that it is "the Lord Jesus" we are honoring. The name of deity is "Lord"; His human name, "Jesus." By this observance we remember the death of the One who became the bridge between God and man, the Redeemer for whom Job cried. It is He who placed one hand on the throne of holiness and the other upon a lost race. As we remember Him, the scenes of His agony, suffering, and death are pressed upon our hearts. We partake, not mournfully, but in the same spirit He Himself manifested. "Looking unto Jesus, the author and finisher of our faith, who for the joy that was set before Him endured the cross, despising the shame, and is set down at the right hand of the throne of God" (Heb. 12:2). It was "when He had given thanks" that Jesus instituted this ordinance. Certainly, for the Christian it is not to be a time of sadness.

We do not approach this observance with fear and trembling. It was designed by our Lord to bring reverent gladness and the highest joy. While receiving the emblems of a sacrifice which God has accepted as totally satisfactory for sin, we are mindful that He has lifted the weakest, poorest believer into a heavenly standing, removing his every spot or stain.

The Lord's table is not only *retrospective,* but also *prospective.* "For as often as ye eat this bread, and drink this cup, ye do show the Lord's death *till He come*" (1 Cor. 11:26). One of the most precious truths of the Word of God is that the Lord will not leave His Church on this earth forever. When we gather at the table of our Lord, we stand between His first and second comings: looking back with gratitude to the One who redeemed us with the shedding of His blood, and looking forward with ardent hope for the appearing of God's Son from heaven. It is the same Jesus who died for us, the Lord Himself, whose coming "draweth nigh." This was the hope of Bishop Bickersteth, who wrote in 1862:

> See, the feast of love is spread:
>   Drink the wine, and break the bread—
> Sweet memorials—till the Lord
>   Call us round His heavenly board:
> Some from earth, from glory some,
>   Severed only "Till He come."

The Manner of Participation (vv. 27-29)

Paul then set down a stern warning: "Wherefore, whosoever shall eat this bread, and drink this cup of the Lord, unworthily, shall be guilty of the body and blood of the Lord. But let a man examine himself, and so let him eat of that bread, and drink of that cup. For he that eateth and drinketh unworthily, eateth and drinketh judgment to himself, not discerning the Lord's body" (1 Cor. 11:27-29).

The Corinthian Christians were eating and drinking at the table of the Lord in an unworthy manner. The word "unworthily" has needlessly terrified many believers, who have thought they could never be worthy to participate in such a sacred event. This term does not have the slightest reference to the unworthiness of the person who comes, but to the unworthiness of the manner of coming.

The Corinthians had turned the memorial of Christ's death into a worldly festival, each taking his own supper before the others could join him. Some were hungry and others drunken. The crux of their wrong conduct is described in the words, "not discerning the Lord's body." They were partaking in an unworthy manner.

What does the Christian see as he sits at the

Lord's table? Just little pieces of broken wafer? Just some grape juice in a cup? If so, he should not partake. These emblems speak of His love to us, and our participation should speak of our love to Him.

Though in Corinth the failure to discern the Lord's body took an ugly and disgraceful form, many transgress as badly today. I have seen Christians treat this feast of love lightly by whispering, drowsiness, and even frivolity. Still others disregard the observance, and think nothing of missing the time of "remembering Him."

An ordinance which was eternally planned in the counsels of the Godhead should have great importance to every believer! Those whom God has invited to the supper, and whom the blood of Christ has made fit to be there, should examine themselves, confess sin, and with whole heart and mind discern the body of the Lord.

Chastening (vv. 30-32)

When a believer allows sin in his life to go unconfessed and unjudged, he will be chastened by the Lord. The Corinthians were guilty of such unconfessed sin, and God's chastening took the form of sickness and death. This judgment was necessary, not because they were not Christ's own, but because they *were*. The Apostle Paul said, "But when we are judged, we are chastened of the Lord, that we should not be condemned with the world" (v. 32). God chastens His children in various ways. It may be by adversity (Psalm 94:12-13). Sometimes it is by sickness as is mentioned here. Or, as was the case with David, it may be with sorrow (2 Sam. 12:15-23).

The Corinthian church was undergoing the chastisement of God. Many were weak and sickly, and many had died. Their particular sin was the ignorant and willful abuse of the Lord's table. But this or any other unjudged sin may cause the unbeliever, now as well as then, to experience the chastening hand of God. We are living in an "unspanked age." Chastening is resented, whether it be in the home or in the school. Too often the current and mood of the age has filtered into the Church. But the Word of the Lord is sure, for it says, "For whom the Lord loveth He chasteneth, and scourgeth every son whom He receiveth. If ye endure chastening, God dealeth with you as with sons; for what son is he whom the father chasteneth not?" (Heb. 12:6-7)

Christians must not assume that all sickness, weakness, and death are the result of God's chastening hand upon His children. Not at all! But every Christian should examine himself, not in morbid self-scrutiny, but in the light of God's revealed Word, and ask himself, "Am I discerning the Lord's body? Is there unconfessed, unjudged sin in my life?" Paul's words should be seriously weighed and honestly applied by every believer.

But you might ask, "Do you mean that God actually caused the death of some Christians in Corinth because of their carelessness?" Yes, He did! The Apostle John verified this when he wrote, "If any man see his brother sin a sin which is not unto death, he shall ask, and he shall give him life for them that sin not unto death. There is a sin unto death; I do not say that he shall pray for it. All unrighteousness is sin, and there is a sin not unto death" (1 John 5:16-17).

A much-used servant of the Lord once said, "It

has been my habit for years to spend the last half hour before I go to sleep in looking over the day, asking God to let me see where wood, hay, and stubble have found incorporation in my life building. I would ask Him to judge me then and there, and to burn up the wood, hay, and stubble, that nothing may stand but gold, silver, and precious stones." This self-examination and self-judgment produces purity of life and deliverance from sin.

Many Christians may right now be under the chastening hand of God because of unjudged sin. They need to confess their transgressions, and be assured that this gracious promise of our Lord is true: "Now no chastening for the present seemeth to be joyous, but grievous; nevertheless, afterward it yieldeth the peaceable fruit of righteousness unto them who are exercised by it" (Heb. 12:11).

As we approach the end of this present age, let us increasingly "remember Him." In what better manner could we do so than by meeting with those who are members of the Body of Christ, and by showing "the Lord's death till He come."

I recall a night when I boarded a train to ride to a destination several hours to the south. I anticipated meeting with the young lady I loved. I was met at the station and we drove to her home. In my coat pocket was a little box that contained an engagement ring. Late that night I placed the ring on her finger as a pledge that one day I would return to take her as my bride. In the intervening time, I suppose she looked often at that sparkling circle upon her hand and thought, "Soon we shall be together." That ring was a promise that our anticipation would soon come to fruition.

Our blessed Lord has given to His Bride, the

Church, an engagement ring. When we gather around the table in communion, we remember Him "till He comes." Joy should fill the heart of the Bride, for that memorial pictures the price paid for salvation, and points forward to a completed redemption in the presence of our Heavenly Bridegroom! The Marriage of the Lamb will then be consummated, and His Bride will find eternal fulfillment in the One who "loveth us, and washed us from our sins in His own blood" (Rev. 1:5).

If you have been slighting the blessed memorial of communion, correct this conduct immediately. If you are failing to discern the body and blood of the Lord in partaking of the elements, right now confess this sin.

May the Church of Jesus Christ ever remember her Lord with grateful praise and expectant joy, knowing that "unto them that look for Him shall He appear the second time without sin unto salvation" (Heb. 9:28).

11

Body Building

1 Corinthians 12:12-31

On a Saturday morning I entered the parking lot of a shopping plaza. Standing in line at the door of a certain establishment was a group of men attired in warmup suits and tennis shoes, waiting for opening time. They were part of a vast army that frequents the spas and health clubs of our land. They were involved in the popular business of "body building."

God is also involved in building a Body, but of quite a different nature—the Church. This Body, of which Christ is the Head, began at Pentecost, and was ushered in by a great diffusion of gifts of the Spirit. They came in accordance with an Old Testament prophecy, for Peter said that they were a fulfillment of the words of Joel (Acts 2:16). These Spirit gifts, initially demonstrated in Jerusalem, extended to all classes of people in the church and were marked by a great diversity. Without doubt, some of them were also given to members of the Corinthian church. But instead of a positive effect, there came confusion, jealousy, pride, and possibly even a counterfeiting of some of the gifts. The "body," which should have been developing in strength and stature, was experiencing division, dissatisfaction, and envy.

To correct this situation, Paul wrote "concerning the spiritualities." The Corinthian church had been cursed with carnality. The members of that congregation needed to return to the things of the Spirit, and reject the things of the flesh. Far more important than building up the physical body was the development, growth, and operation of the Church, the *Body of Christ.*

This most descriptive term, which speaks of the relationship of the risen, glorified Christ to the Church was also used in Paul's epistles to the Ephesians. He said that God put all things under His feet, and "gave Him to be the head over all things to the church, which is His *body,* the fullness of Him that filleth all in all" (Eph. 1:22-23). Then in Ephesians 5:30 he said, "For we are members of His body, of His flesh, and of His bones." This same word is also used in the Book of Romans: "For as we have many members in one body, and all members have not the same office, so we, being many, are one body in Christ, and every one members one of another" (12:4-5). The Christians in Corinth needed to know and practice the meaning of this truth. So do we.

One Body (v. 12)

The Apostle reached one of the mountain peaks of divine revelation when he said, "For as the body is one, and hath many members, and all the members of that one body, being many, are one body, so also is Christ" (v. 12). The illustration is the human body. If Paul had said, "So also is the church," we would not be surprised. But note those last four words, "so also is *Christ*." This is one of the places in Scripture where all believers collectively are called "Christ." Paul had received the germ of this truth on the road to Damascus when he fell to the earth and heard a voice say to him, "Saul, Saul, why persecuteth thou Me?" (Acts 9:4) He had been persecuting Christians, not realizing that in so doing he was persecuting Christ. He would one day learn that every believer is a member of Christ's body.

The psalmist declared concerning his physical body, "For I am fearfully and wonderfully made" (Ps. 139:14). A chemist estimated that the average 150-pound body of a man contains only enough chemicals for the following: lime enough to whitewash a small chicken house, sugar to fill a small sugar bowl, and about enough iron to make a 10-penny nail. The material substance of the human body is not worth very much, yet this is the very stuff of which a wonderful organism is formed. We are nothing, worthless, unless the Spirit of God has worked upon us, and we have become part of Christ's body and His life. And as the Body of Christ, the church is an organism whose life, unity, and growth are dependent upon the resources of its risen Head, the Lord Jesus.

Baptism by the Spirit (v. 13)

When did the Church begin? How was it formed? How do we become part of it? When the Lord Jesus said in Matthew 16:18, "I will build MY church," He spoke of an organism that was still future. If the Church was started prior to the cross, it has no Saviour. If the church has its inauguration after Christ's death but before the resurrection, it has no living Head. The incarnate Lord was the "corn of wheat" which was to fall into the ground and die. The resurrection brought forth the fruit, and the risen, glorified Christ is now head of the Church.

But how and when was the body formed? The Lord Jesus told His assembled disciples just before His ascension, "For John truly baptized with water; but ye shall be baptized with the Holy Spirit not many days from now" (Acts 1:5).

During the week of His crucifixion He had said, "It is expedient for you that I go away; for if I go not away, the Comforter will not come unto you; but if I depart, I will send Him unto you" (John 16:7). As long as the Lord Jesus was upon the earth, and until after the ascension, the Holy Spirit would not come. Following His resurrection, Christ again reminded His disciples of His promise, using the word "baptize" to speak of the descent of the Holy Spirit. Then, at Pentecost, the baptism of the Spirit took place, and a new age began—the Church Age —which will conclude at the return of the Lord Jesus Christ.

Pentecost was the fulfillment of the Old Testament type in Leviticus 23, the Feast of Wave Loaves. Also called the Feast of Pentecost, it was observed exactly 50 days after the Feast of First Fruits. The Bible states in 1 Corinthians 15:23 that the Feast of First Fruits prefigured the resurrection of the Lord Jesus. Exactly 50 days after the resurrection of Christ, the Holy Spirit descended on the believers waiting in Jerusalem. Thus we read, "And when the day of Pentecost was fully come" (Acts 2:1). The Holy Spirit came on schedule! On that day He initiated the work He came to do. The 120 believers in the upper room were the infant Body which the Spirit of God entered. After Christ had ascended to be glorified in Heaven, He sent down the Holy Spirit to form the church. So, the Church began at Pentecost.

God is continuing to form the Body during this dispensation. At Pentecost the disciples were made members of one body by the baptism of the Spirit. Every Christian since that time has received the same baptism of the Holy Spirit into the Body of Christ, the church. The Apostle Paul says, "For by one Spirit were we all baptized into one body, whether we be Jews or Greeks, whether we be bond or free; and have all been made to drink into one Spirit" (1 Cor. 12:13).

By this baptism, therefore, everyone who believes on the Lord Jesus is placed into the Body of Christ. Notice that many carnal Christians were included with those to whom Paul spoke in Corinth. Some of them, even though having experienced the baptism, were guilty of partisanship, divisions, disorders at the Lord's table, and even immorality. The baptism of the Spirit, therefore, is not some experience which causes a Christian to be superspiritual or endued with special power to exercise spiritual gifts. It makes us members of the Body of Christ. A. J. Gordon said, "The upper room became the Spirit's baptistry."

The epistles are filled with statements that the believer is "in Christ." God sees us as having died, having been buried, and having been raised with the Lord Jesus. These positive descriptions of our present standing suggests the negative side of our former condition. There was a time when we were *not* in Christ. Positionally, we were in Adam, dead in trespasses and sins. But now we are alive from the dead spiritually, having received forgiveness. We are in Christ through our union with Him, which took place when we believed on Him. At that same moment, the Holy Spirit baptized us into the Body of Christ, the act of which Paul spoke when he said, "For by one Spirit were we all baptized into one body" (v. 13).

Diversities (vv. 14-26)

The Corinthian believers had been added to the Body of Christ by the same Spirit who had united the waiting believers in the upper room. But the Spirit is also the One who bestows spiritual gifts. Christians at Corinth either did not know this truth or were ignoring it. The gifts of the Spirit extended to all classes of people, young and old, rich and poor, learned and illiterate. It was He who "divideth severally as He will." These very gifts, exercised in the apostolic era, were marked by great diversity. Paul again employed the metaphor of the body he had used in verse 12. This time he went into detail, indicating how the various members of the body function, and how ridiculous it would be for jealousy to arise between them. The foot, the hand, the ear, the nose—each has its purpose and place.

Even seemingly unimportant members have an important function. The members of our human bodies have all been assigned a specific task by an all-wise God. The same is true in the Body of Christ, the Church. Verses 14 and 20 state the same principle from two different angles. Reading those verses carefully and pondering their meaning should make us realize anew that Christ is Head of the Church, and that every believer, as a member of that Body, has a unique function to perform.

In verses 14 through 26 of this chapter the Apostle gave four admonitions which indicate how believers are to live as members of this body.

1. Do not belittle yourself (vv. 15-17). What striking questions are contained in these verses! When you hear the foot "complaining" about not being the hand, and the ear "grumbling" about not being the eye, and both of them deciding that they are not of the body, you're reminded of many Christians today. I have heard numerous times, and so have you, some self-deprecating believer lamenting, "If only I had the talents of Mrs. So-and-so," or "If I just had the opportunities Mr. So-and-so has had, I could do something for the Lord." How much better to accept ourselves as we are, and do our best to serve God with the talents we have.

Recognize, Christian friend, that you have been made alive in Christ. You are indwelt by the Holy Spirit. The Apostle Peter said, "As *every* man hath received the gift" (1 Peter 4:10). How foolish for the foot, because it has a different function from the hand, to say, "Because I am not the hand, I am not part of the body." But Christians sometimes engage in such foolishness. No doubt this was the case at Corinth.

2. Do not deprecate others (vv. 20-24). No member of His Body can say to another, "I have no need of you." We are mutually related and interdependent, just as the members of the human body.

Again consider the analogy. The least attractive and least public members of the body are often the most needed for its existence.

I think of a host of sweet, lovely Christians across this land whose names will never appear on the title page of a book, whose voices will never be heard from a public platform and whose influence may be considered by other believers to be of no consequence. Some of them are reading this chapter right now. The faithful prayers and sacrificial stewardship of God's people like this have made possible the effective proclamation of the Word of God by Radio Bible Class over the years. Theirs is an important function in the Body of Christ.

We must increase in our knowledge and application of this vital truth: Christians need one another. There is no aristocracy of believers. Each is a member of Christ's Body, and each has his part to perform. True, the sovereign Holy Spirit has given some members gifts that appear more prominent than others. But these members cannot function effectively without the supporting activity of those whose ministry is veiled and unobserved by human eye.

At the end of World War II, General Eisenhower received many plaudits for his great accomplishments in defeating the Axis Powers. But he responded by giving the credit and praise to his staff, realizing that without the dedicated, selfless work of his aides, and the tireless efforts of thousands of behind-the-scenes people, victory would not have been possible. And the same is true in the Body of Christ. Back of every great work that is done for the Lord are many unseen believers whose prayer and dedication make it all possible.

3. Acknowledge God's appointment and oversight (vv. 18, 24). God has done two important things for the Church. First, he has "set the members, every one of them, in the body" (v. 18). The Lord Jesus had said to His disciples, "Ye have not chosen me, but I have chosen you, and ordained you [or "appointed" you] that ye should go and bring forth fruit, and that your fruit should remain" (John 15:16). The Greek word *ordained* is the same word that is translated "set" in verse 18 of our chapter. He has therefore "set" or "appointed" the members in the Body. Second, He has "tempered the body together" (v. 24). This means that He has adjusted or attuned the members of the Body, so that they will function together smoothly.

4. Be concerned and cooperative (vv. 25-26). The Apostle also calls for unity within the Body. "That there should be no schism in the body, but that the members should have the same care one for another. And whether one member suffer, all the members suffer with it; or one member be honored, all the members rejoice with it" (1 Cor. 12:25-26). It's important to the health of our physical bodies that each member function in cooperation with every other member, and in direct response to the head. How much more so to the Body of Christ! When, as in Corinth, there are divisions, schisms within the body, what pain is brought to the entire body and to its Head, the Lord Jesus Christ! As a member of the Body of Christ, each Christian has the inescapable responsibility to care for the spiritual health of other members, and to be careful of his own well-being. The body is often judged by the action or the appearance of one member. The world cannot see the

mystical union between the Christian and Christ, but it does see the effects. "By this shall all men know that ye are My disciples, if ye have love one to another" (John 13:35).

Remember, God hath "set the members, every one of them, in the body, as it hath pleased Him." May we as members of the Body of Christ so live that we will bring pleasure to the Heavenly Father who appointed us, and praise to our glorified Head, the Lord Jesus.

Christian friend, you are important to Christ and His Body! Failure to exercise your gifts, refusal to function as an individual member, and selfish and uncooperative attitudes which divide the Body— all these bring displeasure and hurt to the Lord Jesus. And the Body itself is weakened. May our desire for the Church be that of the Apostle to the believers at Ephesus: "But, speaking the truth in love, may [we] grow up into Him in all things, who is the head, even Christ; from whom the whole body fitly joined together and compacted by that which every joint supplieth, according to the effectual working in the measure of every part, maketh increase of the body unto the edifying of itself in love" (Eph. 4:14-16).

12

Signs That Cease

1 Corinthians 13:8-13

The religious news article began, "It didn't register on the Richter scale, but a sharp jolt shook up the fifty delegates and other participants at last month's fifth annual meeting of the scholarly Society of Pentecostal Studies. . . . The jolt came not through a new upper-room visitation of the Spirit but in a banquet talk by the main speaker. . . . [He] challenged his audience of the old-line or 'classic' Pentecostals and modern-day charismatics to abandon the use of tongues. . . . [He] nevertheless declared that the modern use of tongues is a 'mistaken bypass' based on a misunderstanding of Scripture. He maintained that glossolalia in the New Testament refers to known dialects, not unknown tongues. . . . Concluding that there is 'no evidence of [such] religious glossolalia in the New Testament, the early Church, or in history,' [the speaker] called on Pentecostal leaders to 'use intellectual honesty responsibly to face this misuse'" *(Christianity Today,* January 2, 1976, p. 37).

The problem this speaker raised was not the same problem being confronted in Corinth. There had been the abuse of spiritual gifts, marked by carnality and disorder in the assembly. Yet the Apostle could say of that church, "Ye come behind in no gift." Continuing the theme taken up in chapter 12, Paul did not discourage the desire for the best gifts, but showed that there was something better than anything he had mentioned in that list. As believers, they had been placed by the Holy Spirit into the Body of Christ.

Every Christian is born of the Holy Spirit, baptized with the Holy Spirit, indwelt by the Holy Spirit, and sealed by the Holy Spirit. All four of these occurrences take place simultaneously at conversion. For the Corinthian Christians, and for us, "the love of God is shed abroad in our hearts by the Holy Spirit who is given unto us" (Rom. 5:5). God the Spirit dwells in us and produces Christlikeness, or "the fruit of the Spirit" (Gal. 5:22-23). Predominant in that cluster of fruit is love. So the Apostle said, "But covet earnestly the best gifts; and yet show I unto you a more excellent way" (1 Cor. 12:31). Paul then proceeded to pen the "love chapter" of the Bible, 1 Corinthians 13. He urged these Christians to use diligently the "more excellent way," which transcends any spiritual gift or its use. Love must be the mainspring of all our service. Paul particularly stressed this for the church at Corinth because he saw the time approaching when sign-gifts would be "done away."

The Church today is confronted by a great emphasis on the gift of tongues. Glossolalia, the speaking in tongues, is held by some to be the evidence of the baptism of the Spirit, and by others as the manifestation of the Spirit's fullness. As a result, many sincere Christians are seeking the experience of speaking in tongues, which is neither commanded nor supported by the Bible. The Word of Truth, rightly divided, takes precedence over all experience. If the Scripture teaches that the gift of tongues was a manifestation not only for the apostolic age but also for present church history, then every believer should welcome its display. But if the New Testament teaches by precept and occurrence that this particular sign-gift was *not* intended to be the continuing experience of the church, we dare not ignore the weight of biblical teaching, but must presume that it is no longer in effect.

The Permanence of the Gift

The Lord Jesus, just prior to His ascension, said,
These signs shall follow those who believe: In My name shall they cast out demons; they shall speak with new tongues" (Mark 16:17). The fulfillment and confirmation of this prophecy is recorded in the Book of Acts, and is verified by the writer to the Hebrews: "How shall we escape, if we neglect so great salvation, which at the first began to be spoken by the Lord, and was confirmed unto us by them that heard Him, God also bearing them witness, both with signs and wonders, and with diverse miracles and gifts of the Holy Spirit, according to His own will?" (Heb. 2:3-4)

God did "bear witness" with signs, wonders, miracles, and gifts of the Holy Spirit, as is recorded throughout the Book of Acts. The final chapter gives the culminating exhibition of the Lord's confirmation of the Word with signs. In fulfillment of Christ's prediction, the Apostle Paul was not harmed when bitten by a serpent on Melita. He also laid hands on the sick and they were healed.

Several years prior to this, while the Apostle was in residence at Ephesus, he had stated clearly that certain gifts would be done away with. Writing to the believers in Corinth, he said that "tongues . . . shall cease." Yet, some Christians today, earnest in their desire to serve the Lord, are determined to have this gift and others. They become involved in all sorts of doubtful practices in their desire to obtain them. The confusion that results indicates that this is *not* sanctioned by the Lord.

The Spiritual Gifts

Only two of the lists of spiritual gifts enumerated in the New Testament include the gift of tongues, and both of them are found in 1 Corinthians 12. The first begins with verse 8, "For to one is given, by the Spirit, the word of wisdom; to another, the word of knowledge by the same Spirit; to another, faith by the same Spirit; to another, the gifts of healing by the same Spirit; to another, the working of miracles; to another, prophecy; to another, discerning of spirits; to another, various kinds of tongues; to another, the interpretation of tongues" (1 Cor. 12:8-10).

The second is recorded in verse 28 of the same chapter: "And God hath set some in the church: first apostles, second prophets, third teachers; after that miracles, then gifts of healings, helps, governments, diversities of tongues" (1 Cor. 12:28).

Paul lists the gifts of the Spirit in Romans 12:3-8 and again in Ephesians 4:11-13, where he names the gifted men whom the risen Christ has given to the church. *The gift of tongues is not mentioned in either of these passages!* Were some of the gifts temporary, given only for a set time? To assume that because a certain gift was operative in the apostolic age means that the same gift should be operative today is erroneous reasoning, and is contradictory to the teaching of the Word of God.

Consider the example of the gift of apostleship. Paul said, "God hath set some in the church: first apostles" (v. 28). We have just read from Ephesians 4 that when the risen Christ gave gifts unto men, "He gave some, apostles." Would anyone dare claim this gift today? Could you give me the name and address of an apostle in your church? No! The church recognizes, and rightly so, that the gift of apostleship has ceased. That gift was temporary. We read that we "are built upon the foundation of the apostles and prophets, Jesus Christ Himself being the chief corner stone" (Eph. 2:20).

The apostles were responsible for laying the foundation. That gift was exercised in the first century of the Church's existence. A foundation is laid once, and the superstructure is built upon that foundation. When the foundation was completed and the Scriptures were given to the church, apostleship was ended. No claim of apostleship is valid today, for that purpose has been served. The gift was temporary.

The New Testament does not tell us of any attempt to choose successors for the apostles, though they themselves did appoint one to fill the place of the traitor Judas after the ascension of the Lord Jesus. We read in the first chapter of Acts that an apostle had to be a witness of the resurrection. Paul qualified for this office by being "one born out of due season." With the death of the last apostle, the gift and the office ceased.

The Cessation of the Sign

If one of the gifts noted in 1 Corinthians 12:28 ceased at the end of the apostolic age, and certainly centuries before the conclusion of this church age, we need not be surprised if other gifts, especially sign-gifts, should also cease. Remember, the Apostle Paul said that "tongues are for a sign" (1 Cor. 14:22). By applying the prophecy of Isaiah 28:11-12 he made it doubly clear that tongues were a sign to Israel in their unbelief. He also stated, "Truly the signs of an apostle were wrought among you in all patience, *in signs,* and wonders, and mighty deeds" (2 Cor. 12:12).

We must again bring into focus what the author of Hebrews said about the "so great salvation," which was "spoken by the Lord, and was confirmed unto us by them that heard Him, God also bearing them witness, both with signs and wonders, and with diverse miracles and gifts of the Holy Spirit" (Heb. 2:3-4). The sign-gifts and miracles were the corroboration of the apostles' ministry. When the New Testament Scriptures had been completed and the apostles had died, signs were no longer necessary. The transition period between the crucifixion of the Lord Jesus and the destruction of the city of Jerusalem, foretold in Luke 21, called for these phenomena as confirmation of the message. Only then would revelation be completed, and the evidences are borne out by the witness of the epistles themselves.

John R. W. Stott, writing concerning the gifts of

the Spirit in his booklet *The Baptism and Fullness of the Holy Spirit,* said:

This revelation of the purpose of God in Scripture should be sought in its didactic, rather than its historical parts. More precisely, we should look for it in the teaching of Jesus, and in the sermons and writings of the apostles, and not in the purely narrative portions of the Acts. What is described in Scripture as having happened to others is not necessarily intended for us, whereas what is promised to us we are to appropriate, and what is commanded us we are to obey. (John R. W. Stott, *The Baptism and Fullness of the Holy Spirit,* Inter-Varsity Press, Downers Grove, Ill. 1964, pp. 8-9.)

What is the primary source of truth regarding the Church? We find it in the epistles, and especially the Pauline letters. But the epistles are strangely silent on the matter of speaking in tongues. Only one epistle, 1 Corinthians, speaks pointedly to the subject, and the following chapter of this book explains in detail the situation at Corinth. Glossolalia was not mentioned in 2 Corinthians. There is nothing in the epistle to the Galatians relating to signs and miracles. Ephesians has no mention of the sign-gifts; Colossians is silent. There is not one work of miracles or inclusion of spiritual phenomena in Philippians; and 1 and 2 Thessalonians carry no account or comment of miracles, healings, or tongues. Paul does speak in 2 Thessalonians 2:9 about "signs and lying wonders" at the end of the age, but these will occur in the future, and are "after the working of Satan." The remaining epistles are silent on the subject.

A Temporary Sign
If it had been normal to expect the manifestation

of the gift of tongues to continue through the church age, Paul certainly would have given instructions for its use or made reference to its exercise in his other letters. Is it not strange that in the Epistle to the Ephesians, where we are told the permanent gifts of the Spirit that must abide for the testimony of the Gospel and the edification of the church of Jesus Christ, neither the gift of tongues nor any other of the sign-gifts is mentioned? The reason they were left out is to be found in the purpose for which these miraculous gifts were given. They came at the beginning of the age, and were signs to confirm the Gospel as it was first preached. They are not necessary for the perfecting of the saints, nor for the work of the ministry, nor for the edifying of the Body of Christ, and therefore they were withdrawn.

Church history attests to the cessation of the sign-gift of tongues. Cleon Rogers writing in *Bibliotheca Sacra* said:

After examining the testimony of the early Christian leaders whose ministry represents practically every area of the Roman Empire from approximately A.D. 100 to 400, it appears that the miraculous gifts of the first century died out and were no longer needed to establish Christianity. Furthermore, it is very evident that even if the gift were in existence, in spite of all the testimony to the contrary, it was neither widespread nor the normal Christian experience. The only clear reference to anything resembling the phenomena is connected with the heretic Montanus and those influenced by his erroneous use of the Spirit. All of the evidence points to the truth of Paul's prophecy when he says, "tongues shall cease." (Cleon Rogers, *Bibliotheca Sacra*, April-June 1965, p. 143)

After the Apostle Paul had given the church at Corinth his tremendous exhortation to exercise the gifts in love, he set forth a most striking direct statement concerning the temporary aspect of the gift of tongues. In the very heart of his discussion on the subject he said, "Love never faileth; but whether there be prophecies, they shall be done away; whether there be tongues, they shall cease; whether there be knowledge, it shall vanish away" (1 Cor. 13:8). I recognize that some disagree on the interpretation of this verse, and I would seek to "speak the truth in love." All must certainly agree that the inspired penman said clearly, "tongues . . shall cease." Equally sincere Christians differ as to when, but there is no question that Paul is speaking of the gift of tongues, the gift of prophecy, and the gift of knowledge. It should be understood that the same verb is used in 1 Corinthians 13:8 for both prophecy and knowledge, and that it could be translated "rendered inoperative." But the Apostle Paul says clearly that tongues shall *cease.* We read further, "For we know in part, and we prophesy in part. But when that which is perfect [or mature] is come, then that which is in part shall be done away (rendered inoperative)" (1 Cor. 13:9-10).

The Apostle said that something perfect or mature was coming that would render prophecies and knowledge inoperative. The teaching of verses 8 through 10 is that tongues would cease of themselves, and that prophecies and knowledge would be "rendered inoperative" by the arrival of that which was mature. Of what is the Apostle speaking? Prior to the completion of the New Testament, prophecy and knowledge were partial. Men received messages directly from God and made them known to the people. But this was not His full revelation. When the New Testament was finally completed, prophecy and knowledge were "rendered inoperative." By the omission of tongues in verses 9 and 10, therefore, Paul indicates that this gift would already have ceased before prophecy and knowledge were rendered inoperative. The absence of any reference to tongues in the other epistles is further indication that they were not being experienced.

Not only is the gift of tongues no longer in operation, therefore, but the supposed use of the gift today bears little resemblance to the way the genuine was practiced in the apostolic age. Alden A. Gannett has stated it so well in an unpublished classroom study entitled *A Biblical Approach to the Modern Charismatic Movement.* He writes:

The gift of tongues as produced by the Holy Spirit ceased during the age of the apostles. The question today is *not*, as so many propose, can God bestow the gift of tongues today? Of course He can. Rather, the issue is, has God *purposed* to do so since His purpose for tongues has already been fulfilled? It is most significant that, historically speaking, tongues occurred *only* in connection with the ministry of the apostles, that both this sign and healing and other miracles occurred less and less through the Book of Acts.

Today we rejoice in a completed revelation. Everything God wanted to make known through special revelation has been given in His written Word. The Lord no longer speaks by dreams, visions, and prophecies given through men of our day. He has spoken, and that divine revelation is His Word, both the Old and New Testaments.

The Apostle Paul concluded by saying, "And now

abideth faith, hope, love, these three; but the greatest of these is love" (1 Cor. 13:13). Here is the contrast. "These three" faith, hope, and love, abide through this age; "those three" (tongues, prophecies, knowledge) did not last throughout this age. Prophecies and knowledge became inoperative with the completion of revelation and the end of the apostolic age, and by that time the gift of tongues had already ceased.

God forbid that we should engage in the unscriptural practice of seeking a sign when God has given to us the full revelation of His Son in His Word. Don't forget that when the rich man in hell requested that Lazarus be sent back from that other world to witness to his brethren, father Abraham replied, "They have Moses and the prophets; let them hear them!"

"Ah," he said, "but if one were to go to them from the dead, they would repent!"

The prompt reply came, "If they hear not Moses and the prophets, neither will they be persuaded, though one rose from the dead" (see Luke 16:31). The Scriptures are sufficient.

Every Christian must be willing to bring his experience and life into conformity with the Word of God. We must not seek the spectacular; search the Scripture and find in them all that is needed in knowledge and experience. May our lives be characterized by "faith, hope, and love." Rather than seeking sign-gifts which are already obsolete, let us desire the spirituality which is characterized by the fruit of the Spirit—"love, joy, peace, longsuffering, gentleness, goodness, faith, meekness, self-control."

13

Corinthian Confusion

1 Corinthians 14

Two extremes can be discerned within the Church of Jesus Christ: a cold, dead formalism and a rampant emotionalism. Neither brings glory to God! In recent years a movement known as the charismatic revival with a strong emphasis on glossolalia, or speaking in tongues, has gained wide acceptance. Often in small prayer groups, sometimes in the church services, and frequently in private devotions, this phenomenon has been experienced. We have endeavored in this chapter and the one preceding to "zero in" on the teaching of 1 Corinthians on this subject. After all, no spiritual experience is valid unless it conforms in doctrine and practice to the Word of God.

Sincerity alone does not determine rightness or holiness. Equally well-meaning Christians have sharply contrasting experience, and each may insist that his was of God. If personal experience is regarded to be more important than the teaching of God's Word, however, the Christian stands in danger of delusion, for people's experiences may differ greatly.

Any person who has been born again—made partaker of the new nature and placed in the Body of Christ—is a brother or sister in the Lord. We are expected to have Christian love for every fellow believer. But with this love comes the responsibility of weighing his experiences in the balances of the Word of God.

A certain publication of the modern charismatic movement, sometimes called "the Holy Spirit's renewal," reads as follows:

The historic Christian denominations accept the Bible as the revealed Word of God. Therefore, since speaking in tongues is clearly spoken about in the Bible, Christian people can be assured that this is not a "new teaching": Everything the Bible says about speaking in tongues has always been an implicit part of Christian doctrine. . . . What we are encountering in our day is not a new doctrine, but the experience and practice of a doctrine which we have always implicitly held.

But stop and think about that for a moment! To infer that the practice of speaking in tongues is to be part of the Christian's experience today simply because it is mentioned in the Bible is to fail in correctly interpreting the Word of Truth. It is of utmost importance that we turn to the Bible to learn what it teaches about the purpose of the gift of tongues, and then to decide whether or not that purpose is to be sought after by believers today.

The Purpose of the Gift: A Sign
What was the reason for the bestowal of this gift? Remember, the Apostle Paul penned 1 Corinthians

while he was still living at Ephesus, where one of the three occasions of speaking in tongues recorded in the Book of Acts took place (see Acts 19:1-7). Paul wrote the following words to the church in Corinth: "Brethren, be not children in understanding; however, in malice be ye children, but in understanding be men. In the law it is written, 'With men of other tongues and other lips will I speak unto this people; and yet for all that will they not hear me, saith the Lord.' Wherefore, *tongues are for a sign,* not to them that believe, but to them that believe not . . ." (1 Cor. 14:20-22). The gift of tongues was a supernatural bestowal intended to perform a specific function. Its purpose is stated succintly in this passage: it was "for a sign!"

Evidently the believers in the church at Corinth had misunderstood the reason for the gift of tongues. They gave it undue emphasis in the assembly, thereby showing their immaturity as Christians. Those who claim to have the gift of tongues today betray their lack of scriptural understanding. This in itself should cause us to question the genuineness of that which is claimed to be authentic by the charismatic revivalists.

A Sign to the Jews

In this careful delineation of the function of the gift of tongues, Paul referred to the Book of Isaiah (28:11-12). The historical setting for that passage was the Assyrian captivity of the northern kingdom of Israel, and the subsequent invasion of Judah. At that time the Lord spoke to His covenant people Israel through the language of the Assyrians. The Apostle Paul, by quoting this passage, indicated that it was also a prophecy of the gift of tongues as a sign to the Jewish nation. In 1 Corinthians 14:21 Paul used the expression "this people," and by no stretch of the imagination could this phrase be interpreted to mean anything other than the Jewish nation.

We emphasize again that these signs were for the Jews, not the Gentiles. The writer of 1 Corinthians declares, "For the Jews require a sign, and the Greeks seek after wisdom" (1:22). The Church of Jesus Christ, made up of all true believers, does not need a sign, because its members "walk by faith, not by sight" (2 Cor. 5:7). But if the gift of tongues was intended for unbelieving Jews only, as Paul says, how is this confirmed in the scriptural account? The three instances of speaking in tongues recorded in the Book of Acts clearly reveal that this sign was given for the Jews.

First, on the day of Pentecost, Peter preached to a great multitude who had come together when they heard them speaking in tongues. They were "confounded, because every man heard them speak in his own language" (Acts 2:6). These men were Jews. The speaking in tongues was a sign given to them to confirm (or authenticate) Peter's message.

Second, those of Cornelius' household spoke with tongues, as recorded in Acts 10 where Peter and other Jews were present. Up until then, the Jews had refused to believe that the Gentiles were to receive the Gospel and the gift of the indwelling Holy Spirit. This occurrence of tongues was a sign to confirm this fact to them.

Third, in Acts 19, Paul met 12 men (either Jews or Jewish proselytes) who had received John's baptism. Evidently they did not know of Christ's completed work of redemption, nor of the coming of the Holy Spirit. To authenticate the message of salvation in Christ to these Jews, as well as those in the synagogue in Ephesus, the gift of tongues was again manifested.

The Experience at Corinth

But what about Corinth? Was that use of the gift of tongues also a sign to unbelieving Jews? We read in Acts, "After these things Paul departed from Athens, and came to Corinth . . . And when Silas and Timothy were come from Macedonia, Paul pressed in the spirit, and testified to the Jews that Jesus was Christ" (Acts 18:1, 5). The Jews, however, opposed their message. The city of Corinth was a center of world commerce, and many Jews lived there and maintained a thriving synagogue. But these unbelieving Jews blasphemed and refused the messages they heard from the Apostle Paul, so God confirmed it with a sign—the gift of tongues, exercised by believers in Corinth. Therefore, in each of the three occurrences of tongues recorded in the Book of Acts, and the rightful exercise of the gift at Corinth, Jews were present. This harmonizes with the statemens by the Apostle that God made available the gift of tongues in the apostolic age as a sign to the Jews that the Gospel is true.

The gift of tongues was sovereignly bestowed on some of the Early Church believers, enabling them to speak in languages they had not learned, to confirm the message of the apostles and the Early Church to unbelieving Jews. Several evidences showed that this gift was temporary, was confined only to the apostolic age, and was to precede the completed revelation of the Bible. They were: (1)

the fulfillment of Joel's prophecy by the three occurrences in the Book of Acts; (2) our Lord's prediction that these signs would "follow those who
believed" the message of the apostles; and (3) the
direct statement of Hebrews that it "was confirmed
unto us by them that heard Him, God also bearing
them witness, both with signs and wonders, and
with diverse miracles and gifts of the Holy Spirit"
(Heb. 2:3-4).

To summarize, Paul had written to the Corinthian
church, "Tongues . . . shall cease." The limited
number of occurrences of this gift in the Book of
Acts, the absence of any reference to it in the epistles with the exception of 1 Corinthians, its marked
omission from subsequent church history, and its
doubtful validity since apostolic times—these are
all indications of the temporary and limited purpose of the gift.

The Problem in Corinth

Let us consider the confusion in Corinth, the one
church where the gift was in evidence. Many of its
members had heard the word of the Lord from the
Apostle Paul, for he had ministered in that city for
18 months, "teaching the word of God among
them." In his first epistle to the Corinthian Christians, as we saw in the preceding chapter of this
book, the Apostle enumerates the spiritual gifts that
are to be exercised in the Church. "For to one is
given, by the Spirit, the word of wisdom; to another,
the word of knowledge by the same Spirit; to
another, faith by the same Spirit; to another, the
gifts of healing by the same Spirit; to another, the
working of miracles; to another, prophecy; to
another, discerning of spirits; to another, various

kinds of tongues; to another, the interpretation of tongues" (1 Cor. 12:8-10). In a later verse, a similar list is presented: "And God hath set some in the church: First apostles, second prophets, third teachers; after that miracles, then gifts of healings, helps, governments, diversities of tongues" (1 Cor. 12:28).

The walk of many Corinthian believers was carnal, and all kinds of wickedness had been tolerated in that assembly. Sectarianism and pride were the dominant evils. In both of the texts quoted above, the gift and interpretation of tongues were given a position of minor importance. Yet the church at Corinth was indicating their immaturity by placing too much emphasis on the gifts. The level of their spiritual knowledge was very low indeed. In reality, they were still "babes in Christ." The Apostle Paul therefore devoted a considerable portion of the epistle urging them to correct their sinful practices and instructing them in the faith in Christ which he had first taught them.

Furthermore, glossolalia was never intended for all believers, even in the apostolic age. Paul asked several rhetorical questions in 1 Corinthians 12: 29-30. The answer to each of them is a resounding "NO!" One of these questions was, "Do all speak with tongues?" In their carnal, immature state, they had not grasped the truth of the Body of Christ, and did not realize that each member had an individual function and talent. But even those who were given the sign-gifts in the Corinthian assembly were charged with the edification of the entire congregation and the Body of Christ. This is the meaning of 1 Corinthians 12:7, "But the manifestation of the Spirit is given to every man to profit." This means literally, "is given to each for the common good."

Regulation for Use
The Apostle placed certain regulations or limitations upon the gift of tongues in the apostolic assembly, as indicated in 1 Corinthians 14. These restrictions were:

1. Tongues were for a sign to believers (v. 22).
2. Tongues were to be used for the edification of the church (v. 26)
3. No more than three people in the assembly were to speak in tongues during a service, and each was to speak in turn (v. 27).
4. There was to be no speaking in tongues unless they were interpreted (v. 28).
5. Any confusion or disorder in the assembly was an indication of something that did not originate from God (v. 33).
6. In the apostolic church, women were to keep silent and not to speak in tongues (v. 34).
7. To recognize these regulations as the commandments of the Lord was imperative (v. 37).
8. Though not forbidding tongues in the apostolic assembly, the predominant command was "covet to prophesy" (v. 39).

The confusion and disorder that resulted in the Corinthian church was an indication that their undue emphasis on tongues was not from God. The violations in the apostolic assembly of the eight regulations listed above indicated clearly that the gift was spurious. Christian people today who fail to observe these explicit instructions, yet contend that they have the gift of tongues, are being deceived.

A Word for Today

Believers today are not exhorted anywhere in the Scriptures to desire this gift. Instead, the commands of the Word of God are in the opposite direction. Paul's word to the church at Corinth was, "But covet earnestly the best gifts," or as another translation says, "But earnestly desire the greater gifts." To give prominence to that which the Bible does not is to engage in the same error as the church at Corinth.

The believer must be extremely careful that he does not neglect the Word of God, or fail to obey its regulations. To foster or engage in an emotional exercise presumed to have been originated by the Holy Spirit, when the experience does not have a biblical foundation in either its nature or its purpose, opens the believer to satanic influence and "doctrines of demons." Christians who fall prey to false teaching, allowing their emotions to come under the influence of practices that cannot be substantiated by the Word of God, place themselves on dangerous ground. The Bible commands, "Beloved, believe not every spirit, but test the spirits whether they are of God" (1 John 4:1).

14

Resurrection Reality

1 Corinthians 15

As a Christian was walking through an art gallery in Glasgow, he came upon a small boy gazing intently at a painting of the crucifixion. After watching him a moment, the man laid a hand on the boy's shoulder. "Young fellow," he said, "what is this picture of?"

"Why, sir," said the boy, "don't you know? It is our Lord dying on the cross. He's bearing our sins."

The man patted the boy on the shoulder and said, "Thank you, son." He then walked on, looking at other paintings in the gallery. Suddenly he felt a tug at his sleeve.

It was the boy again. "Pardon me, sir. I forgot one thing. He's not dead anymore. He's alive!"

Just as the heart pumps life-giving blood throughout the human body, so the resurrection of Jesus Christ is the "heartbeat of the Gospel." The raising of Christ from the dead is the pivot upon which all the evidence of Christianity turns. By His resurrection Jesus of Nazareth is proven to be all that

He claimed to be. It is the conclusive proof that He accomplished all that He undertook, that His work is complete, and that His sacrifice is accepted. The Archbishop of Armagh once said, "The resurrection is the rock from which all the hammers of criticism have never chipped a single fragment."

Christ's sacrifice on the cross met all the claims of God's justice. Without His death our salvation would be impossible, for through it God is "just and the justifier of him that believeth in Jesus" (Rom. 3:26). But if Christ had not risen from the dead, His death upon the cross, rather than being the ground of our everlasting salvation, would have been the occasion of our despair. If death had been able to keep Him, sin would not have been conquered. The resurrection is therefore the very basis of the church. Everything hinges upon it. Without it, all else would be vain.

The entire first epistle to the Corinthians is corrective, and chapter 15 is no exception. Perhaps Grecian philosophy had found its way into the church, influencing some to deny the resurrection of the body. Or, there may have been an extension of the belief of the Sadducees, "who say that there is no resurrection" (Matt. 22:23). We today have their counterparts in the modernists, the false cults, and others who deny the physical resurrection of the body. These deadly heresies rob the Christian of his most inspiring hope—the hope of life beyond the grave.

The epistle of 1 Corinthians does not deal with the church as a *heavenly* body. It is more concerned about the place and conduct of the Church *in the world*. How wonderful, however, that at the close of this epistle, we should be lifted to another plane, the realization that we are citizens of heaven! The study of the doctrine of the resurrection will remind us again of our position in Christ, and refresh our prospect of being with Him and like Him.

The Gospel and the Resurrection (vv. 1-4)

Paul begins this great resurrection chapter with a brief but complete definition of the Gospel. He writes, "For I delivered unto you first of all that which I also received, that Christ died for our sins according to the Scriptures; and that He was buried, and that He rose again the third day according to the Scriptures" (1 Cor. 15:3-4).

This is what he had preached when he first arrived, and his message had not changed. Let us make certain that the Gospel which we believe and proclaim is nothing more, nothing less, than this simple definition.

The importance of the Bible is stressed in this passage, for Paul said, "according to the Scriptures." He is referring to the Old Testament types of the death and resurrection of the Lord Jesus. But you may ask, "Where in the Old Testament do you find the resurrection on the third day?" (1) Genesis 22: 4-14 records the heart-rending story of Abraham offering Isaac as a sacrifice upon an altar on Mount Moriah. Isaac was a type of Christ, for we read in Hebrews 11:19, "Accounting that God was able to raise him up, even from the dead, from which also he received him in a figure." (2) We also have these words of the Lord Jesus: "For as Jonah was three days and three nights in the belly of the great fish, so shall the Son of man be three days and three nights in the heart of the earth" (Matt. 12:40).

Jonah's "burial" in that great fish and his subsequent "resurrection," are types of the entombment and resurrection of our Lord. (3) The feast of first fruits, explained in Leviticus 23:9-14, was also a type fulfilled in the resurrection. (4) On the day of Pentecost, Peter quoted these words of the psalmist: "For Thou wilt not leave My soul in sheol, neither wilt Thou permit Thine Holy One to see corruption" (Ps. 16:10). He then said, "For David speaketh concerning Him [Christ]" (Acts 2:25). (5) The great preview of the crucifixion, Isaiah 53, has in its very center the truth of the resurrection, for verse 10 says, "He shall see His seed, He shall prolong His days, and the pleasure of the Lord shall prosper in His hand."

Witnesses to the Resurrection (vv. 5-7)
Paul gives evidence for the resurrection by marshaling an impressive array of witnesses. Most of them were still living, and they could not be successfully contradicted. Like a good attorney, he lists them in order:

1. *He was seen by Peter* (v. 5). What a sweet witness of unforgetting love! The one who had dishonored the Lord by his denial was brought out of his despondency by seeing the risen Saviour. Luke's Gospel tells us that Peter had the privilege of being the first apostle to see Christ after He came forth from the tomb.

2. *He was seen by the twelve* (v. 5). All of the disciples saw Christ after His resurrection. Even the skeptical Thomas, when he saw His visible wounds, could only say in belief, "My Lord and my God" (John 20:24-29).

3. *More than 500 brethren saw Him at one time*

(v. 6). This is the only mention of this event in Scripture. It very likely took place in Galilee. The Lord had made a special appointment to meet His disciples there, and just that hint would have caused many more of His followers to be present. Note that the Apostle adds, "The greater part remain until this present time, but some are fallen asleep [are dead]." No possibility of a conspiracy to make up a story! Imagine trying to get 500 false witnesses together, and persuading them to tell the same story!

4. *He was seen by James* (v. 7). This was probably a reference to the half-brother of the Lord Jesus. It had been said shortly before, "Neither did His brethren believe in Him," and this included James. But this man, who was to become a leader in the church at Jerusalem, was changed by the resurrection from disbeliever to a disciple.

5. *He was seen of all the apostles* (v. 7). Many Bible scholars believe this refers to that final gathering at Olivet when Christ was taken up to Glory. They not only saw the risen Christ, they witnessed His ascension into Heaven.

Paul's Personal Witness (vv. 8-11)

Paul now adds his own experience to the witness of these other men. One commentator wrote, "When the number of the apostles might seem to have been closed, and from the midst of those who were filled full with Jewish enmity, Christ was seen by Paul himself, a notable witness of divine grace, the grace that he above all, was to be the witness of." (F. W. Grant. *(The Numerical Bible:* Acts through 2 Corinthians, New York: Loizeaux Bros, 1901 p. 525) The One Paul met on the Damascus road had changed his life. None could deny this. Ananias said, "Brother Saul, the Lord, even Jesus, that appeared unto thee in the way as thou camest, hath sent me" (Acts 9:17).

The witnesses Paul mentioned, therefore, and he himself, were in agreement: they had seen Christ alive. What convincing proof of the resurrection!

The Importance of the Resurrection (vv. 12-19)

The Corinthian believers had not denied the resurrection of Christ. It was part of the Gospel, and they had believed it. But now some of them, incredibly, were denying the future resurrection of their own bodies. Paul therefore gave seven arguments to show that the resurrection of Christ and the resurrection of the believer's body are inseparable truths. He argues that if the believer's body is not to be raised:

1. Then Christ is not risen. This is a logical deduction. One is inseparably linked to the other.

2. All preaching is vain, for there is no Gospel apart from the resurrection of Christ. Our message is robbed of life; our preaching is emptied of its good news. Its note of joy is gone; it has become a funeral dirge. If Christ is not risen, the angels lied on the night of His birth when they said, "Behold, I bring you good tidings of great joy." If Christ is not risen, our preaching has lost its impact, and our Gospel becomes just the history of a man who failed.

3. Paul and all the apostles were false witnesses. They all had preached the resurrection. If Christ is not risen, these representatives of God were guilty of deceit. And if this is the case, then all scriptural authority breaks down, and we are adrift

on an ocean of doubt with no star, no pilot, no com
pass.

4. Faith is vain. The trust that men and women
have in Him is empty. If Christ is not risen, your
hand reaching out in faith has grasped nothing.
You did not receive life, pardon, and deliverance.
Your faith is a delusion if He is not risen.

5. We are all still in our sins. Peter, addressing
the Sanhedrin, said, "Neither is there salvation in
any other; for there is no other name under heaven
given among men, whereby we must be saved" (Acts
4:12). If Christ is not risen, there is no more saving
efficacy in His name than in the name of Plato or
Socrates or Mohammed. The "old account" you
thought was "settled long ago" is still on the books
and unpaid.

6. The dead in Christ have perished. When Paul
said to the bereaved Christians at Thessalonica,
"Wherefore, comfort one another with these words,"
he spoke a useless admonition if Christ be not risen.
How often in the years of my ministry in the pastorate did I follow the funeral train to the silent city
of the dead. I have read, as I stood beside the open
grave, the words of the Apostle from the last portion of this chapter and from the fourth chapter of
1 Thessalonians. But if Christ be not risen, those
words were useless, and the ones we have "loved
long since and lost awhile," are lost forever.

7. Christians are the most miserable persons on
earth. Paul himself is an illustration of this, for he
had turned from a life of ease and affluence to one
of hardship and persecution.

But wait! Don't end the paragraph! Don't put in
a period until with the Apostle you have cried out,
"But now *is* Christ risen from the dead!" Our faith

is not a mirage, not a fantasy. The suppositions of verses 13 through 19 are mere speculations. "Christ *is* risen!"

Order of Events (vv. 20-28)

The Apostle then related the resurrection of Jesus Christ, and all subsequent resurrections, to the program of God.

First, he went back to the beginning of human history. We can review man's past with the words, "In Adam all die." That sums it up! That is the story of mankind, the descendants of the first Adam.

An old Scottish theologian said, "So fully are all individuals represented, that we may say that there have been but *two persons* in the world, and *two great facts* in human history." Those two persons are Adam and Christ, the first Adam and the last Adam. The two great facts he referred to are *death* in the sin of the first Adam, and *resurrection life* in the last Adam, the Lord Jesus.

Paul explained the order of the resurrection:

1. Christ the first fruits (v. 20). Leviticus 23:9-14 gives the particulars of the feast of first fruits. A man representing Israel went out in the field, cut a sheaf of newly ripened grain, and brought it to the priest, who waved it before the Lord "on the morrow after the sabbath." That sheaf of grain spoke of a coming harvest. Mark 16:1 says of the resurrection, "When the sabbath was past." Matthew's Gospel puts it this way: "In the end of the sabbath, as it began to dawn toward the first day of the week." The Lord Jesus, the great wave sheaf, came forth from among the dead in fulfillment of this Old Testament feast, and in pledge that an

abundant harvest is coming in the resurrection of believers.

2. All who believe in Christ. Verse 23 says, "Christ the first fruits; afterward they that are Christ's at His coming." This is the next scheduled event on God's prophetic calendar. We read of it in verses 51-53 of this chapter, and in 1 Thessalonians 4:16-17. The dead in Christ will rise first, then living believers will be "caught up" to join them with Christ in the air. Revelation 20:4 says that they "lived and reigned with Christ a thousand years."

How the Dead Are Raised (vv. 35-37)

After establishing that the resurrection of Christ is a pledge of the raising again of the believer's body, and after giving the order of the resurrection, Paul answered this question: "How are the dead raised up?" The philosopher can only speculate, for his wisdom stops on the burial side of the grave. Divine revelation, however, begins at the resurrection side, and carries us into the eternal ages. Paul anticipated two questions: "How?" and "What?"

What happens to a body that is placed in the grave? It goes back to dust. To reassemble that body in the resurrection seems impossible to our finite minds. Only God's Word has the answer. Faith does not set reason aside; faith supplements reason.

The Apostle answered the questions with an illustration from the farm. Grain sown into the ground seems to decay, but the farmer knows that it will bud and bring forth the same kind of grain. Likewise, a wonderful transformation has been prearranged by God for His children. Our Lord said, "So is the kingdom of God, as if a man should cast seed into the ground; and should sleep, and rise night and day, and the seed should spring and grow up, he knoweth not how. For the earth bringeth forth fruit of itself; first the blade, then the ear, after that the full grain in the ear" (Mark 4:26-28). Since there is order in nature, we may expect order in the resurrection of the body.

Individuality and Improvement (vv. 38-44)

Every seed, though it looks like the others, has its own individuality. Every Christian will retain his individual identity in the resurrection. But our resurrection bodies will differ substantially from our natural bodies. Paul made this clear in four couplets:

1. *Sown in corruption, raised in incorruption* (v. 42). Regardless of what the so-called "faith healers" of today teach, the body is susceptible to corruption. We get sick and die. No matter how much faith a believer possesses, the deteriorating processes are still at work in his body. Only one body did not see corruption: the body of our Lord (Ps. 16:10).

2. *Sown in dishonor, raised in glory* (v. 43). How pitiful is an emaciated body just before death! How dishonored! But believers ". . . look for the Saviour, the Lord Jesus Christ, who shall change our lowly body, that it may be fashioned like His glorious body" (Phil. 3:20-21). A hint of what that body will be like is given in the transfiguration of our Lord recorded in Matthew 17.

3. *Sown in weakness, raised in power* (v. 43). Our new bodies will never need replenishing. No weariness will need to be relieved by sleep. No weakness will hinder our capacity for work and

activity. Think of the power of our Lord's resurrection body! You and I, as redeemed, transformed believers, will have a similar body.

4. *Sown a natural, raised a spiritual body* (v. 44). You say, "Our bodies will be eternal, like ghosts." Oh, no! They will be visible and tangible, but not subject to the laws of nature like our present bodies. Rather, they will be subject to the laws of the Spirit.

Think of our Lord after His resurrection. If He chose to eat, He did, though He didn't need to. He passed through barred doors. He disappeared out of people's sight. Yet He said, "A spirit hath not flesh and bones, as ye see Me have" (Luke 24:39). What tremendous prospects for the child of god!

Image and Immortality (vv. 40-50)

Adam *received* life, and became the progenitor of the human race. One generation begot another, and we bear the likeness of our ancestors. The last Adam, Christ, is "a life giving spirit." Instead of receiving life, He bestows it. Just as we have all born the image of the earthly line, of which Adam was the head, so also believers will one day bear the image of the heavenly line, of which Christ is the Head. "Beloved, now are we the children of God, and it doth not appear what we shall be, but we know that, when He shall appear, we shall be like Him; for we shall see Him as He is" (1 John 3:2). This does not mean that we will all look exactly alike, any more than it infers that we all look alike now. But we shall bear the image of the heavenly.

A Mystery (vv. 51-57)

As he corrected the heresy that had crept into the

church at Corinth by teaching about the first resurrection, the Apostle revealed a "mystery." This was a previously hidden truth now revealed by God the Spirit that not all Christians shall sleep, or die. The word *sleep* refers to the body and not the soul. That all Christians will not die was a new revelation. The same truth is expressed in 1 Thessalonians 4:16-18. Whether we as believers die and are resurrected, or whether we are caught up to meet the Lord Jesus without dying, we shall *all* be changed! He said, "In a moment, in the twinkling of an eye, at the last trump; for the trumpet shall sound, and the dead shall be raised incorruptible, and we shall be changed. For this corruptible must put on incorruption, and this mortal must put on immortality (1 Cor. 15:52-53). In that day, every believer will shout, "O death where is thy sting? O grave, where is thy victory?" (v. 55)

Exhortation (v. 58)

Great doctrinal truths are often followed by a "therefore." We are told what we should be because of what has been done for us. The Apostle told the church at Corinth, beset by carnality, contention, and confusion, to be "steadfast, unmovable, always abounding in the work of the Lord." This appeal is made because they are "in Christ." What less could be expected from blood-bought, saved sinners? After the stinging rebuke, administered lovingly but firmly, the Apostle exulted in the ultimate triumph of the children of God. From the first to the last, salvation demands this triumphant cry: "But thanks be to God, who giveth us the victory through our Lord Jesus Christ" (v. 57).

Indeed, *the Church stands corrected!* But corrected, the church *stands!* And one day the Lord Jesus will "present it to Himself a glorious church, not having spot, or wrinkle, or any such thing; but that it should be holy and without blemish" (Eph. 5:27). May the expectation of that "wrinkle free" presentation produce holiness of life and doctrine now, and the sure, glorious hope of eternity with Christ!

Epilogue

The prospect of eternal life in heaven staggers the imagination of the finite mind. God has chosen to tell us a little about it in His Word, and it will be glorious beyond description.

If you have read this book or portions of it, and you are not a child of God through faith in Christ, I must have this final word with you. You have only the prospect of an endless, eternal separation from God! If you should die without receiving the Saviour, or if He should come to take away His own and you would be left, all hope would be gone.

I therefore plead with you to accept the provision God has made for your eternal salvation—today! Acknowledge that you are a sinner, unable to do one thing to make yourself acceptable to God. Trust the One who died for you and rose again. He has paid for your sins by the shedding of His blood. The Bible says, "But as many as received Him, to them gave He power to become the children of God, even to them that believe on His name" (John 1:12). You too may be part of the heaven-bound company who will meet the Saviour in the rapture and the first resurrection. Amen.